Walking Weekends
Yorkshire Dales

Mark Reid

*30 circular walks from 15 villages
throughout the Yorkshire Dales,
with two walks of varying lengths
from each village – ideal for a weekend break.*

InnWay Publications

Walking Weekends
Yorkshire Dales

© Mark Reid 2005
First Edition September 2005
Reprinted January 2006

A catalogue record for this book is available from the British Library. British Library Cataloguing in Publication Data.

All maps within this publication are based upon Ordnance Survey mapping reproduced by permission of Ordnance Survey on behalf of HMSO © Crown Copyright 2005. Ordnance Survey Licence Number: 100011978

The contents of this publication are believed correct at time of copyright. Nevertheless the author can not accept responsibility for errors and omissions, or for changes in details given. The information contained within this publication is intended only as a general guide.

Walking and outdoor activities can be strenuous and individuals must ensure that they have suitable clothing, footwear, provisions, maps and are suitably fit before starting the walk; inexperienced walkers should be supervised. You are responsible for your own safety and for others in your care, so be prepared for the unexpected - make sure you are fully equipped for the hills.

'The Inn Way' is a Registered Trademark of Mark Reid.

Published by:
INNWAY PUBLICATIONS
102 LEEDS ROAD
HARROGATE
HG2 8HB

ISBN   1 902001 11 7

This book is dedicated to Elvis
...my German Shorthaired Pointer and walking companion.

Thank you to Rachel Gospel, Bernadette and Stewart Reid for
accompanying me on many of the walks.
Special thanks to Matthew Hunt and Chris Wilson.

Front cover photograph: Wharfedale from Top Mere Road
Back cover photograph: Littondale
4-page colour insert photographs
© Mark Reid

Illustrations © John A. Ives, Dringhouses, York.
www.johnaives.co.uk

Typeset, printed and bound by Spectrum Print, Cleethorpes.

CONTENTS

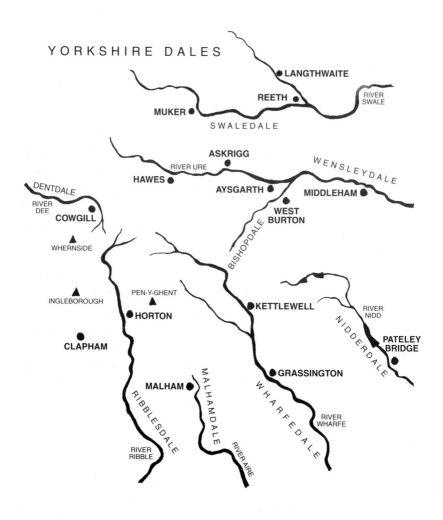

YORKSHIRE DALES

LANGTHWAITE

REETH

RIVER SWALE

MUKER

SWALEDALE

ASKRIGG

RIVER URE

WENSLEYDALE

HAWES

AYSGARTH

MIDDLEHAM

DENTDALE

RIVER DEE

COWGILL

WEST BURTON

WHERNSIDE

BISHOPDALE

INGLEBOROUGH

PEN-Y-GHENT

HORTON

KETTLEWELL

RIVER NIDD

NIDDERDALE

PATELEY BRIDGE

CLAPHAM

GRASSINGTON

MALHAM

MALHAMDALE

WHARFEDALE

RIBBLESDALE

RIVER WHARFE

RIVER RIBBLE

RIVER AIRE

INTRODUCTION

The weekend away is part of the British way of life; a relaxing break that can be taken several times a year to recharge batteries and meet up with old friends. Many people enjoy staying at a traditional country pub and then using it as a base from which to explore the surrounding countryside on foot.

I had arranged to meet our friends on Friday evening at the Sportsman's Inn for two days of great walking. The pub was warm and welcoming, the food and beer delicious and we had found a small table right next to the coal fire. Plates cleared and I spread the OS map across the table, soaking a couple of beer spills up for good measure. The route was planned, although one of the group studied the map in the hope that there was a low-level route to Ribblehead rather than via the summit of Whernside. I assured them that the climb would be worth the effort as the forecast was good and the views would be fantastic.

After a hearty breakfast on Saturday morning, we spent the whole day walking through some of England's finest landscapes with a pub planned for the end of the walk. In the company of good friends for several hours there was time to talk, drink in the scenery and experience the countryside at a gentle walking pace. Things always happen along the way that will be recounted with laughter during the evening... the mishaps, memorable views, wildlife, people you meet and sometimes the weather. Being caught in a storm can be exhilarating, exciting and often challenging.

This is what it is all about. Good English country pubs, convivial company, great food and local ale, superb walks, relaxation and, above all, memories. When you look back at a year that has passed, it is these memories that you think back to; the joy of being alive and standing on top of Whernside looking down at Ribblehead Viaduct with the thought that it is downhill all the way to the Station Inn!

Mark Reid
September 2005

ROUTE DESCRIPTIONS & MAPS

ROUTE DESCRIPTIONS

The following abbreviations have been used throughout the route descriptions:

SP	Signpost	BW	Bridleway
FP	Footpath	FB	Footbridge

The detailed route descriptions and hand-drawn maps should guide you safely round the routes featured in this book, however, always take Ordnance Survey Explorer maps (scale 1:25,000) with you on your walks, as well as a compass. Occasionally, Rights of Way may be altered or diverted to prevent erosion damage or to improve the line of the footpath. Any changes will be clearly signposted and must be followed, and are usually marked on the most up-to-date Ordnance Survey maps.

Footpaths and bridleways throughout the Yorkshire Dales are generally well maintained with good waymarking. The signposts are often colour-coded as follows: yellow for footpaths, blue for bridleways and red for byways. Often, the path on the ground is clearly defined and easy to follow, however, some sections cross remote areas and high moorland where route finding may be difficult, especially in bad weather.

MAPS

The following Ordnance Survey Explorer maps (1:25,000) cover the walks featured in this book.

OL2 'Yorkshire Dales Southern & Western areas'. Lower Wharfedale, lower Littondale, Malhamdale, Ribblesdale and Dentdale.

OL30 'Yorkshire Dales Northern & Central areas'. Swaledale, Wensleydale, Coverdale, Upper Wharfedale and Littondale.

302 'Northallerton & Thirsk'. East Witton, Jervaulx Abbey and Thornton Steward.

298 'Nidderdale'. Pateley Bridge, Brimham Rocks and Nidderdale.

SAFETY

Never underestimate the strenuous nature of walking particularly when this is combined with high ground and the elements. Do not attempt to complete a walk that is beyond your skill, experience or level of fitness.

Obtain a weather forecast before setting out on your walk. If the weather turns bad then turn back the way you have walked. Conditions can change for the worse within minutes making walking hazardous with mist, winds and rain virtually all year round. The weather conditions on moorland can vary significantly from conditions in valleys.

Take Ordnance Survey maps (1:25,000) of the area as well as a GPS (Global Positioning System) or compass.

Your boots are the most important thing; make sure that they are waterproof, comfortable and have good ankle support and sturdy soles.

Waterproof and windproof coat and trousers are essential as well as gloves, hat and fleece for warmth. Travel light as a heavy rucksack can tire you out. Take essential items such as a fleece, snack food, first aid kit, blister plasters, sun cream, whistle, water bottle, torch and 'survival' bag. Drink plenty of fluids (not alcohol) and eat food regularly to keep energy levels up.

Always walk in a group unless you are very experienced and inform someone of your route and report your safe arrival. In an emergency summon help with six blasts of your whistle or call the Police (who will contact the Fell Rescue Team) giving details of the incident and location.

Take care when crossing rivers or roads and walk in single file (facing oncoming traffic) when walking along country lanes. Do not explore old mine or quarry workings.

When walking through grassy moorland keep a watchful eye for adders, Britain's only poisonous snake. If bitten, seek medical help immediately.

Above all, keep your hands out of your pockets and look where you are going! *REMEMBER: "An experienced walker knows when to turn back"*

COUNTRYSIDE CODE

Consider other people
Showing consideration and respect for other people makes the countryside a pleasant environment for everyone – at home, at work and at leisure.

Enjoy the countryside and respect its life and work
We have a responsibility to protect our countryside now and for future generations. Tread gently – discover the beauty of the natural environment and take care not to damage, destroy or remove features such as rocks, plants and trees. Do not touch crops, machinery or livestock.

Leave gates and property as you find them
Please respect the working life of the countryside, as our actions can affect people's livelihoods, our heritage, and the safety and welfare of animals and ourselves. Use stiles and gates to cross boundaries and close gates behind you.

Keep to public Rights of Way or Open Access areas.
Footpaths are for walkers; bridleways are for cyclists, horse-riders and walkers. Motorbikes and cars should keep to roads.

Do not make excessive noise
The hills and valleys should be quiet places

Safeguard water supplies
Streams are used by livestock and often feed reservoirs for drinking supplies.

Guard against risk of fire
Uncontrolled fires can devastate hillsides or moorland.

Keep dogs under control
A loose dog can be catastrophic for ground nesting birds, sheep and sometimes the dog itself. By law, farmers are entitled to destroy a dog that injures or worries their animals.

Take litter home
Litter is dangerous and unsightly.

Safety
Weather can change quickly, are you fully equipped for the hills?

ASKRIGG
Wensleydale

Askrigg ('ash-ridge') dates back to pre-Conquest days and grew as a trading centre as it lay just outside the boundaries of the old Forest of Wensleydale and was therefore exempt from the strict Norman forest laws. A market charter was granted in 1587 and Askrigg developed into an important market town, however, by the turn of the 19th Century the market had lapsed and Hawes gradually began to take over as the 'capital' of the upper dale. It is always a delight to rest on the stone steps of the old Market Cross and look out across the cobbles towards the sweeping main street with its elegant three-storey Georgian houses and imagine the scene on market day all those years ago. Askrigg's heyday was in the 18th & 19th centuries when industries such as lead mining, textile production and clock making flourished. More recently, the village was used as the setting for the TV series 'All Creatures Great and Small' with the Kings Arms doubling as the 'Drovers' whilst the grand three-storey house near the Market Cross was used as 'Skeldale House'. Askrigg church, dedicated to St Oswald, dates from the 13th Century and is the largest church in the dale serving several communities and still retains some original features including lead on its roof from local mines.

THE VILLAGE

Askrigg boasts a hotel, B&B's, general stores and Post Office, delicatessen, café, restaurant, craft shop, public toilets, outdoor pursuits centre and two great pubs.

ACCOMMODATION

National Park Information Centre, Hawes: 01969 666210

ASKRIGG PUBS

Kings Arms, Askrigg   **01969 650258**

This wonderful Georgian building was originally built as a manor house, but later developed into a coaching inn. It is a pub of great character with wood panelling, an inglenook fireplace and old saddle hooks hanging from the ceiling. The pub was used as the 'Drovers Arms' in BBC TV's "All Creatures Great and Small". No accommodation.

Crown Inn, Askrigg   **01969 650298**

This traditional village local is renowned for its wholesome home-made food, good quality ales and friendly atmosphere. An old cast iron range warms one of the small snug areas whilst locals play darts in the other. One of the best pubs in the Dales (in my opinion!). No accommodation.

White Rose Hotel, Askrigg   **01969 650515**

Situated along Askrigg's sweeping main street, this large elegant hotel was built in the 1830's originally as a private house. Inside, there is a traditional bar open to non-residents.

PUBS ALONG THE WALKS

Victoria Arms, Worton   01969 650314
Rose & Crown, Bainbridge   01969 650225

Askrigg Walking Weekend
- Saturday Walk -
Askrigg, Woodhall Greets, Nappa Mill, Worton & Mill Gill Force

WALK INFORMATION

Highlights	James Herriot's 'Darrowby', Askrigg Moor, an old shooters' hut, a fine descent to Woodhall, the village of the foresters, the old Wensleydale Railway, walking alongside the Ure and spectacular waterfalls.
Distance	10.5 miles Time 5 hours
Maps	OS Explorer OL30
Refreshments	Pubs at Askrigg, Bainbridge and Worton. Tea rooms and shops at Askrigg and Bainbridge.
Terrain	A quiet country lane leads up onto Askrigg Moor (steep in places) from where a path leads across open moorland to join another moorland road. A path then strikes off across Woodhall Greets (boggy in places with hidden hollows) before joining a track that leads down to Woodhall. Field, riverside and woodland paths lead to Bainbridge, with a short climb up onto Worton Scar. From Bainbridge, field paths and a country lane lead into the confines of Mill Gill then back to Askrigg.
Ascents:	Woodhall Greets - 530 metres above sea level.
Caution:	The path across Askrigg Moor and Woodhall Greets has few landmarks and is indistinct in places. Take care whilst walking along country lanes and crossing the A684 at Worton. There are steep drops to the side of the path down through Mill Gill.

POINTS OF INTEREST

From Askrigg, a quiet moorland road leads steadily up onto the high ground of Askrigg Moor, bound for Swaledale. On reaching open moorland, our route turns off across heather moorland from where there are superb views back across Wensleydale towards Raydale and Semerwater. High on the windswept moorland of Woodhall Greets are the ruins of Greets Shooting House, a wonderful spot to rest and drink in the scenery. The path then skirts the boggy ground above Beldon Beck before dropping down to Woodhall - this is a superb descent along an old track with Wensleydale laid out before you. The hidden hamlet of Woodhall was once part of the Royal Hunting Forest of Wensleydale as it stands within the former hunting enclosure of Woodhall Park and was home to the Chief Forester of Wensleydale many centuries ago. From Woodhall, the route follows the old track-bed of the Wensleydale Railway to reach Nappa Mill. On the walk back to Bainbridge, make sure you call into the Victoria Arms at Worton (pronounced 'werton') as this is a pub of great character where the landlord is also a farmer, a reminder of the days when most landlords of country inns would have also kept livestock as well as a good pint of ale!

Askrigg was the first village in Yorkshire to be lit by electricity, with power generated by a turbine attached to one of the mill wheels. There were once three mills along Mill Gill, the one our route passes towards the end of this walk was known as West Mill and processed corn. Further up Mill Gill are two spectacular waterfalls, Mill Gill Force and Whitfield Gill Force. This walk takes in Mill Gill Force, where a moorland beck cascades down through a narrow cleft in the overhanging rocks.

For more information about the Wensleydale Railway
please see Walking Weekend 2

ASKRIGG SATURDAY WALK

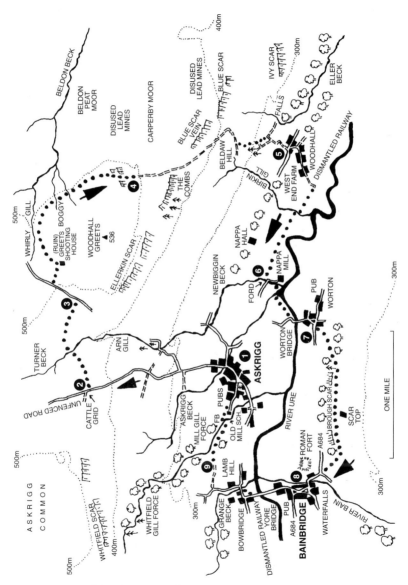

15

THE WALK

1. From the old Market Cross in the centre of Askrigg (with your back to the church) turn left up along the Main Street then take the turning to the left towards 'Muker' just after the Crown Inn. Follow this road up out of the village and follow it climbing steeply up (ignore the turning to the right by the two stone barns) onto Askrigg Common to reach a cattle grid across the road after just over a mile (at the end of the walled road - open moorland in ahead).

2. Turn right immediately after this cattle grid (SP) across the rough grassy / heather moorland alongside the wall on your right at first then gradually bearing to the left away from the wall heading across the rough moorland (no clear path - head towards the corner of the wall on the grassy hillside ahead), down over the small stream of Turner Beck and up to re-join the wall where it bends sharply to the right (*i.e. from the cattle grid, turn right and follow the line of the wall, but cut the corner off by walking across the rough moorland, down over the stream and up to re-join the wall at the corner*). From the wall corner, head on keeping close to the wall on your right to join the unfenced moorland road.

3. Turn left up along the unfenced moorland road for 0.25 miles then take the BW to the right (SP 'Woodhall') and follow the clear path up towards the ruined stone-built shooters' hut on the top of the moorland ahead (Woodhall Greets). As you reach the bottom of the bank immediately below the old shooting hut follow the narrow grassy path up to the left across the moor then follow the clear narrow path as it gradually bends round to the right to reach a bridlegate in a fence across your path (Whirly Gill just down to your left). After the gate, head straight on alongside the old fence-line on your left gradually bending round to the right gently rising up across the moor (keep to the fence-line) to eventually reach a scattering of rocky outcrops at the top of the moor (fence-line becomes a wall on your left), just beyond which the path drops down to a gate in a wall across your path.

4. Head through the gate and follow the grassy path ahead, keeping close to the wall on your left, through a gate after which continue on down along the grassy track (still with the wall on your left) to another gate just below a line of limestone crags/scree slopes. Head through this gate and follow the grassy track straight on down across the field, through another gate then continue straight on then follow the track as it bends quite sharply down to the right winding down Beldhaw Hill passing a lime kiln (with a solitary tree growing out of it) just after which head off the track down to a bridle-gate in the bottom left-hand corner of the field. After the bridle-gate, head straight on down with the wall on your right, over a track across your path (ignore the gate to your right) then down to reach a small metal bridle-gate across your path at the bottom of the field (SP on gate 'Askrigg Moor'). Head through this bridle-gate then continue down to join a rough track where you turn right through a gate (SP 'Askrigg, Woodhall'). Follow the track straight on winding down to reach the road at Woodhall.

5. Cross over the main road and take the lane opposite (road-sign 'Woodhall') and follow this down, bearing round to the right through Woodhall to reach West End Farm at the end of the metalled lane. Continue straight on along the track through the farmyard and follow it down passing some barns to reach an old bridge and the embankment of the former railway line (bridge missing), after which follow the track to the right (SP 'Askrigg') to reach a gate at the end of the track. After the gate head straight on alongside the fence / overgrown railway embankment on your right through a squeeze-stile just after a small stream at the end of this field, after which continue straight on for a short distance then turn right through a metal kissing gate onto the old grassy railway line. Turn left along the railway line and follow it straight on for around 0.5 miles (line becomes more overgrown) until you reach a stile just to the right that leads out onto a field where you continue straight on, now with the overgrown railway line on your left, to reach a gate to the right of a barn that leads onto a farm lane beside an old bridge/ford.

6. Head straight on along the lane (ignore the bridge/ford) down to reach Nappa Mill Farm. As you reach the buildings follow the track to the right of the large corrugated metal barn to reach a gate just beyond (SP). After the gate, head across the field to a FB, after which bear left through a squeeze-stile then left over another FB and follow the riverside path on to reach a wall-gate that leads onto the road. Turn left along the road, over Worton Bridge and up into Worton, bearing to the right along the road to reach the main A684 beside the red 'phone box. *(Short detour to the Victoria Arms that avoids road walking – as you enter Worton at the top of the bank, turn left ('Dead End' sign) then at the end of this lane head straight on along the enclosed path, at the end of which head right up across the field to reach the main road just to the right of the Victoria Arms.)*

7. At the T-junction beside the 'phone box, turn right along the road then left through the second of two gates after 25 yards (SP 'Bainbridge'). Head diagonally to the right up across the field, passing the corner of a fence at the top of the steep grassy bank (SP), then continue on passing the end of a tumbledown wall across boggy ground to reach a squeeze-stile that leads into woodland at the foot of Worton Scar (SP). After the squeeze-stile, head steeply up to the right to reach the top of the wooded scar. Turn right along the top of the wooded scar (SP 'Bainbridge) then out of the woods and continue straight on across flat fields (still with the wooded scar on your right) passing Scar Top Farm across to your left to eventually reach a squeeze-stile to the right in the corner of the field (SP). Drop down heading towards Bainbridge through a series of squeeze-stiles to join the road beside a T-junction with the main A684. Follow this road to the left down into Bainbridge.

8. Walk along the main road across the large village green, bearing right at the junction towards 'Askrigg' and follow this road passing to the right of the Rose & Crown out of the village and down to reach Yore Bridge across the River Ure. Continue straight on up along the road passing beneath the old railway bridge (bridge missing) then take the FP to the right through a squeeze-stile (SP). Head diagonally across

the field (cutting the corner off road) to re-join the road at Bowbridge. Turn right along the road, over the bridge across Grange Beck after which turn left towards 'Helm'. Follow this road climbing up passing Gill Gate farm on your right (with Grange Beck on your left) then, where the road bends up to the left, take the rough track to the right through a gate (SP 'Mill Gill'). After the gate, head straight on along the rough track (keeping close to the wall on your right) across two fields then, as you approach the end of the second field (with woodland ahead of you) bear off the track to the left heading straight on to quickly reach a small wall-gate that leads into woodland.

9. *(Mill Gill Force short detour to the left)* Turn right and follow the clear path heading gradually down, with the steep wooded ravine of Mill Gill down to your left. Follow the clear path down (with the wall on your right), through a wall-gate at the end of the woods, after which head on through another wall-gate just to your left that leads over a FB across Mill Gill. After the FB, follow the clear path to the right alongside the stream then, at the mill buildings, head left beneath the old mill race to a wall-gate. Head through the gate and follow the clear flagged path across a field and through a gate that leads onto a lane. Turn left along this lane and follow it to emerge back in the centre of Askrigg.

Askrigg Walking Weekend
- Sunday Walk -
Askrigg, Bainbridge, Carpley Green, Addlebrough & Thornton Rust

WALK INFORMATION

Highlights	Virosidum Roman fort, climbing the flanks of Addlebrough, the hidden farmstead of Carpley Green, wonderful views across Wensleydale, the hill-village of Thornton Rust and a classic Dales pub.
Distance	9.5 miles Time 4 hours
Maps	OS Explorer OL30
Refreshments	Pubs at Askrigg, Bainbridge and Worton. Tea rooms and shops at Askrigg and Bainbridge.
Terrain	Field paths lead from Askrigg to Bainbridge from where a path heads across the top of Brough Scar to reach Cubeck. A stony track then climbs up across the western flanks of Addlebrough to join a country lane that leads down to Carpley Green. A grassy path (boggy in places) skirts around the eastern slopes of Addlebrough then drops down along a track into Thornton Rust. After about a mile of road walking, a path leads steeply down at first then across fields to Worton from where it is a short walk back to Askrigg.
Ascents:	Worton Pasture - 370 metres above sea level. Thornton Rust Moor - 410 metres above sea level.
Caution:	This walk heads across open moorland on the upper slopes of Addlebrough. The climb out of Cubeck is steep. Take care when crossing the A684 at Worton.

POINTS OF INTEREST

Bainbridge is a delightful village with a large green overlooked by a 15th Century inn. In medieval times this green had an important purpose as a refuge for livestock as the village was then on the edge of the hunting Forest of Wensleydale that stretched from the River Bain to Mallerstang and was home to twelve foresters and their families. The forest was the haunt of wolves and bears and was such a dangerous place to be after dark that a horn was blown each winter's evening to guide travellers to safety - the Forest Horn still hangs in the Rose & Crown. But the history of Bainbridge stretches back a thousand years earlier to the time of the Romans. In about AD80, legions of soldiers pushed northwards from their military stronghold at York to subdue the unruly native Brigantes tribes. A network of roads and forts were built during this period under the supervision of Agricola, Rome's most successful governor in Britain. A fort, known as Virosidum, was built on Brough Hill which rises to the east of Bainbridge. This fort housed up to 500 soldiers who kept a watchful eye on the Brigantes for nearly 300 years, although it was attacked and rebuilt on several occasions. A number of Roman roads were built across the fells to this fort, including Cam High Road that once led across the hills to Ribchester, the course of which can still be seen cutting a straight line up across the flanks of Wether Fell.

There are few hills in the Dales to rival the distinguished splendour of Addlebrough, which stands sentinel above Wensleydale. Its distinctive 'flat-top' profile is instantly recognisable and features in countless photographs and paintings of the dale. Its flat summit plateau, characteristic of many hills in this part of the Dales, is due to the underlying Yoredale series of rocks. This rock strata consists of layers of limestone, grits and shales which are sandwiched together, each type of rock eroding at different rates resulting in the 'stepped' appearance of the valley sides. There are traces of a Brigantes hill-fort on its summit and settlements on its flanks as well as a cairn that is said to be the burial site of an ancient British chieftain called Authulf, who gave the hill its name.

For more information about Semerwater, please see Walking Weekend 6

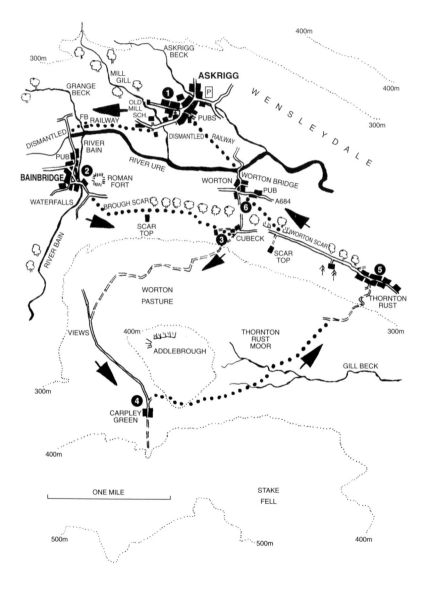

THE WALK

1. From the Market Cross in the centre of Askrigg (with your back to the church) turn right down along the main road and follow this out of Askrigg passing Low Mill Outdoor Centre then take the FP to the left opposite the school (SP 'Yorebridge') over a cattle grid and then cross the stile to the right ahead. After this stile turn immediately right along the fence, passing the old railway station and continue straight on alongside the railway embankment to reach a farmhouse. Pass behind this house (still heading alongside the embankment) and down over a FB across Grange Beck (old railway bridge supports to your right). A flagged path leads on to reach the road at Yore Bridge where you turn left up along the road into Bainbridge.

2. Walk across the large village green (away from the pub) along the main road (A684) towards 'Leyburn & Aysgarth', over the bridge across the River Bain with its waterfalls and on up the hill. Just after you have left the village behind take the road-turning to the right towards 'Semerwater, Stalling Busk' then immediately take the FP to the left through a squeeze-stile in the wall (SP 'Cubeck'). Head up across the field, through a wall-gate to your left after which head up through two more squeeze-stiles onto the limestone ridge of Brough Scar. Turn left alongside the wall across the top of this escarpment (passing Scar Top Farm across to your right) and continue straight on along the top of the wooded escarpment (ignore paths down to the left). At the wall-gate at the end of the woods continue straight on with the wall on your left, then head through the gate on your left (SP) and on passing to the left of the barns to join a farm track. Walk along this track for a short distance then branch off to the right (SP) and head through a gate to the right of the long wooden barn that leads onto a track into the hamlet of Cubeck. Head straight on along this track through the farmyard then where it emerges from the farmyard and opens out at a 'junction' of tracks (but about 50 yards before you reach the metalled road) turn to the right back on yourself along a stony track up through a double metal gate.

3. Follow this clear walled track climbing quite steeply up onto the grassy moorland (Worton Pasture) to reach a gate across your path. Head through the gate and continue up along the track across open pastures up to a second gate across your path (with Addlebrough ahead of you). Head through this gate then turn sharp right along the now level but indistinct grassy track to another gate, after which follow the track across the flat shoulder of land gradually bearing round to the left to join Carpley Green Road through a gate (views of Semerwater ahead). Turn left along this road and follow it down for 1 mile to reach the isolated farm of Carpley Green.

4. As you approach the farm buildings take the bridleway to the left through a gate (SP 'Thornton Rust') immediately before the stone barn on your left. Head through the gate and follow the grassy track up with the wall on your right then round to the right through another gate, after which head straight on bearing up to the left (ignore the track immediately up to the left) along a clear narrow path which skirts around the 'shoulder' of Addlebrough. The clear path leads on through two wall-gates (second gate missing) along a clear path and then heads through a gate in the wall on your right. After this gate, turn immediately left along a clear path (with the wall on your left) across a small 'ridge' and follow this down to reach a gate / ladder stile in a wall across your path *(ignore the permissive path to the left to Addlebrough)*. After this gate / ladder stile, continue straight on along the clear path across the undulating boggy moorland, down to reach a metal gate. Head through the gate and continue on down to join a track across your path (SP). Turn right and follow this walled track winding down to reach the road in the centre of Thornton Rust.

5. Turn left along the road and follow it out of the village. Continue on along this country lane for about 0.75 miles, passing Thornton Lodge Nursing Home, then take the FP to the right (SP 'Worton') through a squeeze-stile just before the entrance to Scar Top Farm. After the stile, drop down through the narrow 'cleft' in the rocks to the left, then steeply down through the woods and out onto a field -

as you emerge onto the field take the path immediately to the left through a squeeze-stile. After this stile, head on through the wall-gap ahead then bear to the right to a squeeze-stile in the far corner of the field, after which head down to the right across the next field to a wall-gate hidden away in the far bottom corner. After this wall-gate, bear across the field to the right and through the large gap in the wall (beneath the small wooded bank) then head on through a series of squeeze-stiles down to reach the main road at Worton.

6. Turn left along the road (take care) then take the first turning to the right into the heart of the village and follow this road down to reach Worton Bridge across the River Ure. Immediately after the bridge, take the FP to the left (SP 'Askrigg') and follow this clear flagged path up to reach the old railway track-bed. Cross over this old railway line and head up the path to the left and follow this up to join a lane, which you follow round to the left into Askrigg.

Askrigg

AYSGARTH

Wensleydale

The village of Aysgarth lies on a shelf of land high above the confluence of Bishopdale and Wensleydale, half a mile from Aysgarth Falls with its trio of delightful waterfalls where the Ure tumbles over shelves of limestone set in a wooded gorge. The view from the western end of the village is superb with Upper Wensleydale stretching away into the distance and the conspicuous landmark of Lady Hill, with its windswept copse of pines, rising proudly above the heart of the valley. The village itself is an interesting mixture of old stone houses set back from the main road behind a narrow green, complete with an unusual war memorial lamp standard. At the western end of the green is a very rare Edwardian rock garden, which has been recently restored. This was commissioned in 1906 by wealthy local landowner Frank Sayer Graham and built by the famous York alpine nursery of James Backhouse & Son with limestone rock feature and waterfalls.

THE VILLAGE

Aysgarth boasts B&B's, shop, tea rooms, garage, Edwardian rock garden and the George & Dragon. At Aysgarth Falls there is the National Park Information Centre, toilets, large car park, café, B&B's, St Andrews Church, the Yore Mill craft shop and a large campsite nearby.

ACCOMMODATION

National Park Information Centre, Aysgarth Falls: 01969 662910

AYSGARTH PUBS

George & Dragon, Aysgarth   01969 663358
This prominent roadside pub lies at the heart of the village. Inside, it has plenty of character with a cosy bar warmed by a log fire, bric-a-brac on the walls and low beams. It has a good reputation for food.

Palmer Flatt Hotel, Aysgarth Falls   01969 663228
This historic hotel stands on the foundations of a medieval hospice for pilgrims, its unusual name comes from the palm branches brought back by pilgrims from the Holy Lands. The present building dates from the 18th Century.

PUBS ALONG THE WALKS

George Inn, Thoralby	01969 663256
Fox & Hounds, West Burton	01969 663111
Bolton Arms, Redmire	01969 624336
Wheatsheaf Hotel, Carperby	01969 663216

Aysgarth Walking Weekend
- Saturday Walk -
Aysgarth, Flout Moor Lane, Stake Road
& Bishopdale

WALK INFORMATION

Highlights	Wild moorland, isolated farmsteads, a superb 'green lane' across Stake Fell, wonderful views of Bishopdale, Thorold's farm and the hidden valley of the Welsh.
Distance	9 miles Time 4 hours
Maps	OS Explorer OL30
Refreshments	Pubs and shops at Aysgarth, Thoralby and West Burton
Terrain	From Aysgarth, a quiet lane then a stony track (Flout Moor Lane) heads up across Aysgarth Moor to reach the isolated Gayle Ing Farm - the final section leaves the track and heads across rough moorland (Haw Head) to reach this farmhouse. The path drops steeply down over a stream then heads up to join the grassy track of Stake Road, which is followed steadily down to Thoralby - the final section is stony underfoot and quite steep. After a short section of road-walking, field paths lead to West Burton and then across more fields (riverside & meadowland) up to Aysgarth.
Ascent	Stake Road - 410 metres above sea level
Caution	This walk climbs up onto rough open moorland, with a number of quite steep descents and ascents. Take care when crossing the road at Newbiggin.

POINTS OF INTEREST

From Aysgarth, an old stony walled track known as Flout Moor Lane leads steadily up across Aysgarth Moor through a wild landscape of rough pastures and open moorland. All around are far-reaching views across Wensleydale towards Bolton Castle whilst across to the east the distinctive flat-topped bulk of Penhill rises above the valley. Just off this track is Castle Dykes Henge, a rare Neolithic henge that dates back some 4,000 years. Oval shaped with an enclosing ditch and bank, archaeologists believe that this was used as a meeting place, trading centre or religious site rather than a defensive fort. Flout Moor Lane eventually leads up to the isolated farmhouse of Gayle Ing, which lies in a sheltered hollow surrounded by trees, with only rough tracks leading up to it - is this the most remote farmhouse in the Dales?

After negotiating the deep gill of Gayle Ing Beck, our route joins Stake Road, a wonderful grassy track that provides a high-level route to and from Bishopdale. This ancient route joins up with the Stake Moss road high above Cragdale, a tributary of Raydale, which itself follows the line of the Roman road that once connected the fort at Ilkley with Bainbridge. Stake Road is now the preserve of walkers and horse-riders, the descent along which affords wonderful views across the deep wooded valley of Bishopdale, Wensleydale's largest tributary - it is quite surprising to see how high you have actually climbed up! During medieval times Bishopdale was the hunting preserve of the noblemen of Middleham Castle. Middleham's ownership and influence came to an end in the early 17th Century, which resulted in a period of house building in Bishopdale, and throughout the Dales as a whole, as many former tenant farmers acquired their holdings and built themselves large stone farmhouses with their new found wealth; Bishopdale boasts some of the finest examples in the Dales of 17th Century yeoman farmhouses. Thoralby lies hidden away in this beautiful valley, first settled by the Vikings as this was 'Thorold's farm'. It is an oasis of peace and quiet with old stone cottages clustered around an attractive green.

For information about West Burton, please see Walking Weekend 15.

AYSGARTH SATURDAY WALK

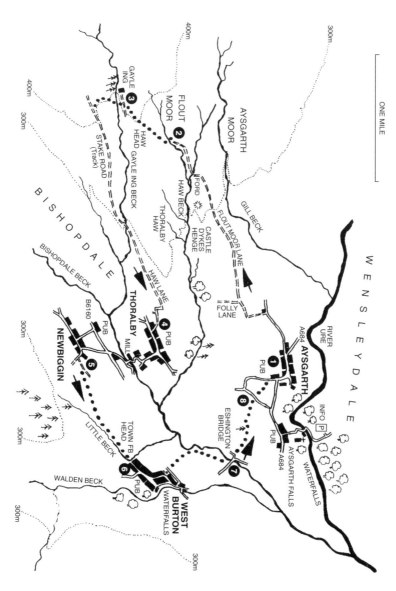

THE WALK

1. From the centre of Aysgarth, head along the main road through the village towards 'Hawes' (keep to the left-hand side of the road) then, where the main road bends sharply down to the right at the top of the village, take the turning straight on to the left (road-sign 'Thornton Rust'). Follow this road out of Aysgarth then, after about 0.5 miles, take the walled stony track to the left just before a stone barn on the corner (SP 'Thoralby, Gayle Ing'). Follow this track rising up then levelling out and bending sharp right then, where the track forks, head along the right-hand walled track bearing slightly to the right (Flout Moor Lane) and follow this for about 0.5 miles to reach a gate at the end of the enclosed track. Head through the gate and continue straight on along the stony track, with a wall on your left and open fields to your right, to soon reach another gate, after which the track becomes enclosed by walls again. Continue straight on up along the walled track (passing Castle Dykes Henge in the field just across to the left after 0.25 miles) gradually rising up for 0.5 miles then bending down to the left over a ford across Haw Beck then bending to the right climbing up again (track becomes rougher underfoot) to reach a gate across your path at the end of the walled track.

2. Head through the gate and continue straight on along the rough grassy track, keeping close to the small stream on your left, then after a short distance follow the track to the left over a ford across this stream and through a wall gate (gate missing). After the gate, follow the grassy track to the right heading up alongside the wall on your right at first then, where this wall bends gradually away, continue straight on along the rough grassy track climbing up across the moorland of Haw Head on to reach a squeeze stile beside a gate in a wall just before the farmhouse of Gayle Ing hidden in trees.

3. Head through the squeeze-stile (SP 'Thoralby') then walk straight on over the grassy farm-track then bear slightly to the right dropping steeply down to reach a FB across Gayle Ing Beck, after which head through another squeeze-stile then bear to the right climbing steeply up to a bridle-gate in a wall at the top of the hill (SP). Head through the bridle-gate then follow the clear narrow path straight on across the heather moorland then bearing round to the left to join the wide grassy unenclosed track of Stake Road across your path running across the ridge of land. Turn left along this track down to quickly reach a gate in a wall. Head through the gate and follow the wide grassy track straight on, with a wall on your right, gently dropping down the hillside through two more gates after which the track becomes a clear stony walled lane. Continue along this lane straight on dropping gradually down for about a mile (views of Bishopdale) then turning sharp right winding steeply down to reach the road at Thoralby beside Town Head Farm. Turn left along the road to reach the George Inn.

4. Just after the pub, take the road turning to the right passing the old Methodist Chapel on the corner and follow this road down out of the village, bending round to the right then left down to reach the Old Corn Mill and a road-bridge across Bishopdale Beck. After the bridge, follow the road to the right (SP 'Kettlewell') up to the crossroads with the main road. At the crossroads, head straight over along the lane opposite up into Newbiggin then, where you reach a T-junction in the village, turn left along the lane (SP 'West Burton, Walden') which quickly becomes a rough track.

5. Follow this track out of the village passing East Farm, after which continue up along the walled rough track climbing up then, where the track divides, follow the clearer track that bends round to the left and levels out. Follow this walled track on then, where it bends slightly to the left, head through the red metal gate to the right. Walk straight on rising slightly up across the hillside through a squeeze-stile ahead, after which head on through another squeeze-stile in the right-hand corner of the field then follow the path straight on across several fields and through a succession of squeeze-stiles gradually bearing very slightly to the right up across the

hillside at first and then straight on across the wide ridge of land until you reach a junction of paths (SP) just to the right of a stone barn. At the barn follow the FP straight on alongside Little Beck on your right through several wall-gates to reach a gate and small FB that leads into the farmyard of Town Head Farm. Walk through the farmyard and follow the road down into West Burton.

6. Follow the road down across the village green, bearing left at the house in the middle of the green passing the pub on your left and then the village shop and follow this road out of the green. Continue along the road as it winds down through the village then take the FP to the left through a gate in between Lenny Garth Barn and The Reading Room (opposite Meadow Croft). Follow this path down to reach the main road. Cross over the road and take the path opposite (SP 'Eshington Bridge') that leads across a field passing to the left of a barn then on through two squeeze-stile in the far right-hand corner of the field (beside Bishopdale Beck). After these stiles, follow the path to the right across two fields to reach a road just to the right of Eshington Bridge.

7. Turn left along the road over the bridge just after which take the turning to the left (as the road bends to the right) and follow this lane up then, where this lane turns sharp left after a short distance, head straight on through a squeeze-stile (SP 'Aysgarth Crossing'). Head straight on with the wall on your left through another squeeze-stile, after which head steeply up the grassy bank passing through the gate to the left of a barn then continue climbing up (with the wall on your left) to reach a gate in this wall in the top left corner of the field. After the gate, head diagonally to the right up across the field (ignore the large gap in the wall at the top of the field) to reach a small squeeze-stile in the top far corner of the field by the top of the belt of trees. After this squeeze-stile, head on to reach a small wall-gate just to your left after which turn right down to reach a crossroads of paths in the corner of the wall at the bottom of the 'hollow'. Head straight on through the wall-gate in the corner of the wall (SP 'Aysgarth') and head straight up the hillside

ahead then, just after an old wall across your path (as you approach the small barn ahead), head right through a wall-gap. After this wall-gap, head across the field bearing slightly left through a wall-gate in the centre of the wall across your path that leads onto a lane.

8. Turn left then almost immediately right through a squeeze-stile (SP 'Aysgarth') and head straight on across the field through a squeeze-stile then follow the path bearing to the left across the next field, through a squeeze-stile to your left, after which head straight on to a wall-gate in the bottom corner of the field that leads onto a lane on the outskirts of Aysgarth. Turn right along the lane to quickly reach the main road which you follow to the left back into Aysgarth.

Aysgarth Church

Aysgarth Walking Weekend
- Sunday Walk -
Aysgarth Falls, Thoresby Lane,
Bolton Castle, Oxclose Road & Carperby

WALK INFORMATION

Highlights	Spectacular waterfalls, ancient coppiced woodland, old lanes and lost villages, Wesley's oak, the castle that held Mary Queen of Scots and wonderful moorland tracks.
Distance	9 miles Time 4 hours
Maps	OS Explorer OL30
Refreshments	Pubs at Aysgarth, Aysgarth Falls, Redmire and Carperby. Tea rooms / shops at Aysgarth Falls, Redmire and Castle Bolton.
Terrain	From Aysgarth, this walk follows woodland paths passing the Middle and Lower Falls, before crossing farmland to reach Hollins House Farm. An old 'green lane' is then followed, enclosed by hedgerows, to join the road at Redmire, from where paths lead up alongside the old railway line then across fields to Castle Bolton. A clear track (stony, then grassy) heads across low moorland before dropping steeply down into Carperby. Field paths lead back to Aysgarth.
Ascents	Oxclose Road - 315 metres above sea level
Caution	The decent from the moorland track into Carperby is quite steep in places. This walk crosses two small fords, which may be difficult after heavy rain.

Aysgarth Falls are set in a beautiful wooded gorge with a fine view of the Upper Falls from the ancient Yore Bridge that spans the river. These waterfalls are spectacular to say the least, particularly after heavy rain, with the river cascading down across huge shelves of limestone falling some 150-ft in the space of three-quarters of a mile. A beautiful riverside walk leads through the ancient woodland of Freeholders' Wood to reach the Middle and Lower Falls. This is a remnant of the ancient woodland that once covered much of Wensleydale with many native species of deciduous trees including rowan, oak, elm, wild cherry, holly and hazel. For centuries, the wood has been managed on a rotational coppicing basis where trees are cut back to ground level, new shoots allowed to grow to a useable thickness and then harvested; the people of Carperby have traditionally held the coppicing rights. It is now owned and managed by the National Park Authority.

An old grassy lane hemmed in by overgrown hedgerows leads from near Hollins House Farm to Redmire via Low Thoresby Farm. Thoresby is one of the lost villages of Wensleydale first settled by Vikings over 1,000 years ago as this was 'Thor's farmstead'. During medieval times this was a thriving village, however, by the early 15th Century the village had disappeared. There are hundreds of deserted medieval villages in this country, the result of a variety of factors including climate change, disease or a greedy landlord! The name of Thoresby lives on in two farms and the old lane that once led to the village.

Redmire is, at the time of writing at least, at the end of the line of the Wensleydale Railway. Completed in the 1870's, this railway once connected the East Coast mainline at Northallerton with the Settle and Carlisle Railway at Garsdale Head until it was closed to passengers in 1954, although the tracks remained between Northallerton and Redmire to service nearby quarries. After concerted effort, passenger trains returned to Wensleydale in summer 2003 and there are plans to extend the railway to eventually join back up with the Settle and Carlisle Railway. A maze of narrow lanes converge on the village green in the centre of Redmire where you will find the famous (but gnarled) Wesley oak tree, where he is reputed to have preached during the 18th Century.

The imposing fortress of Bolton Castle looms above as you approach the village of Castle Bolton. Completed in 1399 by Sir Richard Scrope, the walls of this stout castle soar some 100-ft up to the battlements on the four corner towers. The Scrope family came to Wensleydale in the early 12th Century and held important positions; indeed, Sir Richard was Lord Chancellor of England to Richard II. The castle has witnessed a number of pivotal moments in English history. Mary, Queen of Scots was imprisoned here in 1568 before being taken to Tutbury Castle. During the English Civil War the castle was a garrison for Royalist forces, before surrendering to Parliamentary forces in 1645. In 1647 Cromwell ordered the castle untenable and it remained uninhabited for almost three centuries; the weakening of the structure in 1647 contributed to the collapse of the north-east tower during a storm in 1761. After his release from the Tower of London in 1653, Charles Powlett married the owner of the estate - the castle is still owned by the same family. The present Lord Bolton and his family live at Bolton Hall a little further down the valley. To avoid confusion , the village is called Castle Bolton whilst the castle is called Bolton Castle!

From Bolton Castle, an old track known as Oxclose Road leads high above Wensleydale with wonderful views across the wide valley; this was once the main road through Wensleydale. An old stony track leads steeply down into the village of Carperby, with its old stepped market cross set on a small green. This was where the Wensleydale breed of sheep originated and the real life James Herriot spent his honeymoon at the Wheatsheaf Hotel in the 1930's.

For more information about Aysgarth Church, please see Walking Weekend 15

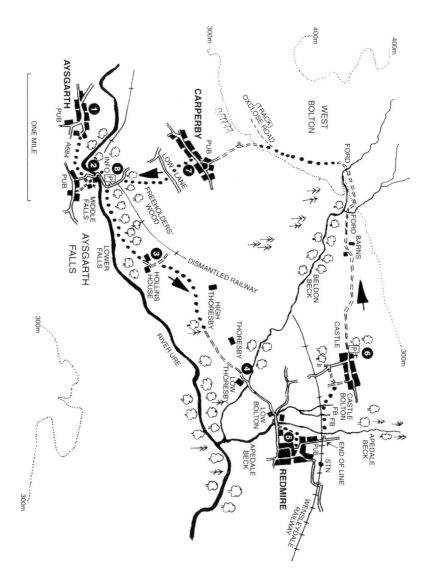

THE WALK

1. From the centre of Aysgarth, head along the main road through the village towards 'Leyburn' then, at the top of the village where the road forks (at the War Memorial lamppost), follow the left-hand lane ('Dead End' sign) down to reach a gate at the end of the lane beside Field House (SP 'Aysgarth Falls'). Head through the gate then up alongside the wall on your right and through a squeeze-stile after which turn left along the enclosed path to reach another squeeze-stile. Continue straight on across several fields through a succession of stiles to eventually reach the road opposite the entrance to St Andrew's Church. Walk straight on through the churchyard to reach the church tower where you turn left through the churchyard then down a flight of steps passing to the side of Yore Mill to reach the road at Yore Bridge above Aysgarth Falls (Upper Falls).

2. Cross the bridge and follow the road to the right then, as the road bends up to the left, take the path on the right ('Middle and Lower Falls') and follow this clear path through Freeholders' Wood passing Middle Falls. Continue on along the path through the woods then down some concrete steps to the right towards the Lower Falls and through a bridle-gate then, where these steps bend to the right (as you reach the steep wooded riverbank - SP 'Lower Falls Viewing Point') follow the path to the left through the trees to quickly reach a stile over a fence at the end of the woods (SP 'Castle Bolton'). Head straight up the hillside to reach a fence across your path, where you turn right (SP 'Castle Bolton') alongside the fence to reach a small wall-gate at the end of the field. Continue straight on along the clear path gently rising up through a gate after which the path becomes a track that leads up to Hollins House Farm.

3. As you reach the farmyard follow the lane to the right passing the farmhouse on your right then continue along the stony farm lane leaving the farm behind then, after about 100 yards where the lane

bends to the left, take the path to the right through a gate (SP). Follow the clear wide grassy path straight on and over a wall stile, after which head on across the field bearing very slightly to the left down to reach another wall stile at the bottom of the field. Do not cross this stile but turn right (SP 'Castle Bolton') alongside the wall on your left and follow this to reach a gate in the bottom corner of the field, after which head straight on with the wall now on your right then, where this wall bends away, continue straight on ('Castle Bolton') along a clear grassy path to soon re-join the wall on your right that leads on to reach a stile beside a gate at the top of a walled overgrown track (Thoresby Lane). Follow this enclosed path straight on all the way to reach Low Thoresby Farm and a metalled lane.

4. Head straight on along the lane (passing behind the farmhouse) down to reach a T-junction with the main road at Low Bolton (edge of Redmire village). Turn right along the road over a bridge across a stream then on over another bridge across Apedale Beck immediately after which turn left (SP) along a track and over a stile beside a gate (Apedale Beck just to your left). Follow the track up for a short distance then, where the track disappears, bear to the right across the field to join the wall on your right. Head up along side the wall on your right and through a squeeze-stile in a 'dog-leg' in this wall, after which turn right through another squeeze-stile then head straight on through a farmyard and through another squeeze-stile beside a barn that leads into Redmire.

5. Turn left along the lane passing the phone box on your left and the village green on your right then turn left and follow the road passing the Bolton Arms pub on your left up out of the village. Follow the road up passing beneath the railway bridge across the road, immediately after which turn left along a track (SP). Follow this track to quickly reach a FB across Apedale Beck, after which continue straight on alongside the railway embankment on your left across two more small FBs. After the third FB, follow the path up to the right through a wall-gap (Bolton Castle in the distance) after

which bear to the left across two fields (through wall-gaps) to join a grassy track across your path which you follow up to the right to reach the road in the centre of Castle Bolton. At the road, turn left through the village then follow the lane to the right behind the Castle to reach a gate at the end of the metalled lane (car park on your right).

6. Head through the gate and follow the stony track straight on (SP 'Askrigg') through a series of gates to reach a group of large wooden barns after 0.75 miles. Continue along the stony track passing to the left of the large barns to reach a gate in a wall across the track, after which continue straight on along the clear track alongside the wall on your left and follow this track turning sharp left through a gate in this wall. After this gate, follow the track to the right down over a rocky ford over a small stream (often dry) and up to reach another gate in a wall (at the end of the clear stony track - open grassy moorland ahead). Head through the gate and follow the wide grassy track bending to the left, keeping fairly close to the wall to your left, heading across the rough open grassy moorland. After a while, the wall on your left ends (with the small valley of Beldon Beck down to your left) - carry straight on along the grassy track then follow it bending round to the left down over a rocky ford across Beldon Beck (often dry) and straight on up to a gate in a wall (SP 'Askrigg, Carperby'). After the gate, carry straight on along the wide rough grassy track bearing very slightly to the left ahead (ignore grassy track immediately to your left alongside the wall) heading across the flat shelf of land (rough terrain) for 0.5 miles to reach another gate in a wall (SP 'Carperby, Askrigg'). Head through this gate then, where the track forks after a few paces, follow the left-hand track alongside the wall on your left and follow this dropping quite steeply down (becomes a sunken track) to join a clear stony track. Follow this track to the left straight on down towards Carperby. As you reach houses on the outskirts of Carperby the lane forks - follow the right-hand lane down to reach the main road where you turn right to reach the Wheatsheaf Hotel.

7. Take the FP to the left through a gate directly opposite the Wheatsheaf Hotel (SP 'Aysgarth') and head down alongside the wall on your right then, halfway down the field, head through a squeeze-stile to your right (SP 'Aysgarth') then continue down across the field with the wall now on your left to reach a squeeze-stile that leads onto a narrow walled lane (Low Lane). At the lane, take the FP opposite to the right through a squeeze-stile (SP 'Aysgarth') then, after about 150 yards, head right through a squeeze-stile (SP) after which continue on along the clear path bearing to the right across the middle of the field, through a wall-gate then carry on through two more squeeze-stiles to reach Freeholders Wood. As you enter the wood, follow the clear path to the right meandering through the woods to reach the road. Turn left along the road then right just after the railway bridge up into the National Park Centre car park.

8. Walk across the car park to join a path at the far end, which you follow down to the left to reach the road at Yore Bridge above the Upper Falls. Cross Yore Bridge then head back up the steps to the side of Yore Mill and through the churchyard to reach St Andrews Church where you turn right along the wide path to reach the main entrance gates to the churchyard and the road. Cross over the road and take the FP opposite through a squeeze-stile (SP 'Aysgarth village') and re-trace your steps straight on across several fields through a series of squeeze-stiles then along a short section of enclosed path at the end of which cross the stile to the right down to reach a gate to the left of a house. Head through the gate and follow the lane bending up to the left back into Aysgarth.

CLAPHAM

Ribblesdale

Clapham is an attractive village surrounded by mature woodland with old stone cottages facing across the tree-shaded waters of Clapham Beck, spanned by several ancient bridges including the narrow packhorse bridge known as Brokken Bridge. Clapham was first settled by Saxon farmers and developed into a commercial centre for the area gaining a market charter in 1201, although the market is now a distant memory. The village was the home to James Faraday the village blacksmith, father of Michael Faraday the pioneer of electrical science whose discoveries helped develop the electric motor. Clapham is largely an estate village developed by the Farrer family who came to this area in the late 18th Century and bought the shooting rights on Ingleborough as well as various farms thus creating a large estate. They built Ingleborough Hall in the early 1800's, planted many trees and created a large lake along Clapham Beck. A philanthropic family, they developed much of the village, built tunnels through the woodland and even provided the village with electricity generated from a turbine near the waterfall along Clapham Beck. Ingleborough Hall is now an Outdoor Education Centre, although the family still lives in the village and own the Ingleborough Estate.

THE VILLAGE

Clapham boasts a railway station (just over a mile from the village), B&B's, cafés, toilets, large car park, craft shop, village shop, Post Office, outdoor shop, Organic farm shop and a pub.

ACCOMMODATION

Tourist Information Centre, Ingleton: 015242 41049

CLAPHAM PUBS

New Inn, Clapham: **015242 51203**
This 18th Century coaching inn has a lovely setting overlooking Clapham Beck. Inside, there is a dining room, comfortable wood-panelled lounge bar as well as a Main Bar. Note the collection of caving cartoons on the walls by Jim Eyre, a local caver. The HQ of the Cave Rescue Organisation is next door.

PUBS ON THE WALKS

Game Cock Inn, Austwick: 015242 51047

Clapham Walking Weekend
- Saturday Walk -
Clapham, Gaping Gill, Ingleborough, Sulber & Long Lane.

WALK INFORMATION

Highlights	The dramatic ravine of Trow Gill, England's most famous pothole, the highest hill-fort in the country, old green lanes and the limestone pavements of Moughton.
Distance	10.5 miles Time 5 - 6 hours
Maps	OS Explorer OL2
Refreshments	New Inn and tea rooms at Clapham; refreshments available at Ingleborough Cave (seasonal). No other facilities along this walk - take provisions with you.
Terrain	Stony paths lead up through Clapdale and Trow Gill (short scramble over boulders) to reach Gaping Gill. A long climb then ensues along a pitched-stone path for most of the way (steep in places) up onto the summit of Ingleborough (exposed to the elements). The descent initially follows a steep path before a clear rocky path heads across the upper flanks of Simon Fell dropping gradually down to reach a junction of tracks at Sulber Nick. Grassy / stony tracks lead back to Clapham.
Ascents:	Ingleborough: 724 metres above sea level
Caution	This is a strenuous walk to the summit of Ingleborough, with rough paths and some steep sections - do not attempt this walk in bad weather. Take a compass and OS map with you. Danger - keep well away from Gaping Gill as there is a 340-ft sheer drop. Limestone is slippery when wet.

POINTS OF INTEREST

The climb from Clapham via Gaping Gill to the summit of Ingleborough is by far the easiest route to the top. The path is clear and well-trodden for most of the way, and the climbs are not as steep as those from Ingleborough's northern or western approaches, however, it is still a strenuous mountain walk up onto the roof of Yorkshire and as such must be treated with caution and respect.

Reginald Farrer was famed for his plant collecting expeditions during the late 19th and early 20th centuries bringing back over 100 new species including Farrer's gentian. Hailed as 'the father of English rock gardening', his books led to the Edwardian fashion for rockeries. The Ingleborough Estate Nature Trail (small fee) was established in 1970 to commemorate Reginald and leads from the old Sawmill at the top of the village passing the large lake that was built in the 19th Century to provide hydro-electric power for the sawmill as well as many houses in the village, Ingleborough Hall and even the street lights - this was the first system of its kind in North West England dating back to 1893. The turbines are still used for some Estate work. The Nature Trail is a delightful walk through the wooded valley of Clapdale Beck with a profusion of wild flowers, mature trees and rhododendrons. Clapdale boasts a mixture of alkaline and acid soils as the Craven Fault cuts across this valley so providing both limestone and gritstone soil conditions. The Nature Trail leads up to Ingleborough Cave, which was opened up in 1837 by the Farrer family who drained an underground pool so allowing exploration of the vast underground cave system that was eventually found to link up with Gaping Gill.

From the entrance to Ingleborough Cave a stony track leads up through the spectacular dry limestone gorge of Trow Gill to reach Gaping Gill, England's most famous pot-hole, where the waters of Fell Beck disappear into a small opening in the ground plunging 340-ft into a cavern large enough to house York Minster! Next, the summit of Ingleborough beckons, with a steady climb up onto the ridge of Little

Ingleborough before the final push for the summit plateau. The views from its north-eastern edge are superb with the Howgill Fells, Whernside, Pen-y-ghent, the Irish Sea, Lakeland and Ribblehead Viaduct in view. Ingleborough is the second highest mountain in the Dales with its two sister mountains of Whernside (736m) and Pen-y-ghent (694m) clearly visible from its summit. Ingleborough is capped by a layer of millstone grit which sits on a layer of shales and sandstones which in turn lies on a huge shelf of Great Scar Limestone, the rock that dominates the scenery in this area. It is these different layers of rock that give the mountain its stepped appearance. The flat summit plateau is encircled by a large tumbledown wall, which form the extensive remains of an Iron Age fort, the highest of its kind in the country used by Venutius, the Brigantes leader, in the 1st Century AD as his headquarters to resist the advancing Roman legions.

A clear path leads from Ingleborough across the flanks of Simon Fell to reach the extensive limestone terrain of Sulber and Moughton, the finest upland limestone pavements in England. At Sulber Gate, there are splendid views across Thieves Moss, with its unusual limestone pavement weathered into a maze of clints and grikes, towards the extensive pavements and scars of Moughton at the head of unfrequented Crummackdale. This is walking country par excellence with springy turf beneath your feet and expansive views.

CLAPHAM SATURDAY WALK

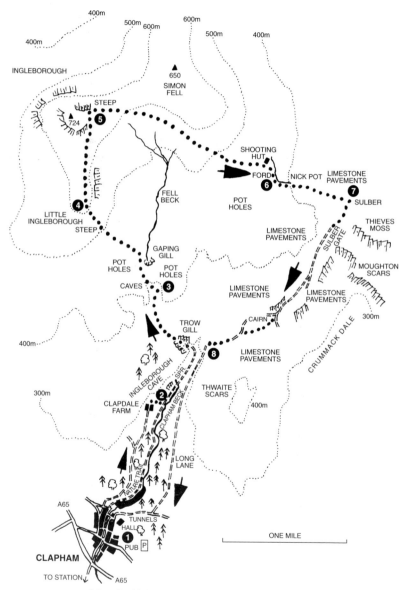

48

1. From the car park at Clapham, turn right along the road heading up through the village (SP 'Ingleborough Cave') then, almost immediately, cross the narrow packhorse bridge to the left (Brokken Bridge) then turn right and follow the road up through the village with Clapham Beck now on your right. Follow the road round to the left at the top of the village (waterfall to your right) passing the private path to 'Ingleborough Cave' then take the walled track to the right (SP 'Ingleborough Cave, Gaping Gill'). Follow this track uphill, passing a wood on your right, to reach a wall-stile beside a gate across the track after about 0.5 miles. Cross the stile and continue straight on along the unenclosed track to reach Clapdale Farm. Follow the path through the farmyard to reach a stile by a gate, after which head steeply down to the right (SP 'Ingleborough Cave') to join the track alongside Clapham Beck, where you turn left to reach the entrance to Ingleborough Cave. *(Alternatively, at the top of the village head through the yard of the sawmill (SP 'Ingleborough Cave'), pay the modest entrance fee and follow the clear track up through the wooded valley of Clapdale to eventually reach Ingleborough Cave).*

2. Carry straight on along the track passing Ingleborough Cave, over the bridge across Clapham Beck (Beck Head spring to your left) to reach a stile beside a gate across the track. Head through the gate and follow the stony track heading straight on up through the dry limestone valley (Clapdale) then curving round to the left to reach a wall-stile beside a gate. Cross the stile then follow the path climbing up through the narrow gorge of Trow Gill, scrambling up boulders through the narrow 'neck' of the valley beyond which the path emerges out into a shallow dry valley with a wall now on your left. Follow the clear path alongside this wall heading up for about 0.5 miles to reach a ladder stile over the wall to your left at the head of the shallow valley (Ingleborough comes into view).

3. Cross the stile then head straight on along the grassy path heading across open grassy limestone moorland (danger - keep to the path,

open potholes) then gently curving round to the right before the path forks - our route heads along the left-hand path heading for the steep southern shoulder of Little Ingleborough ahead *(short detour to Gaping Gill - follow the right-hand path to quickly reach the crater of Gaping Gill. As you approach Gaping Gill, follow the clear path curving round to the left to re-join the Ingleborough path)*. Follow the very clear path bearing to the left away from Gaping Gill before climbing steeply up a stone-pitched path onto the southern rim of the flat ridge of Little Ingleborough (stone wind shelters).

4. Follow the path heading straight on along the eastern rim of this flat ridge, with steep drops sweeping away to your right down towards Fell Beck. After about 0.25 miles the path begins to climb up again, gently at first before a final steep climb up onto the eastern edge of Ingleborough's flat summit plateau. Head straight on along the clear path along the summit plateau's eastern edge to reach the north-eastern corner of the summit plateau above some gritstone crags by a large stone cairn (views towards Whernside directly ahead and Ribblehead Viaduct in the valley bottom).

5. As you reach this north-east corner of the summit plateau, turn right and follow the clear narrow path steeply down the (northern) side of this plateau edge (pitched in places) then, where the path forks halfway down the steep upper slopes, follow the wide right-hand (eroded) path heading steeply down (Pen-y-ghent in the distance). The path soon levels out and leads straight on (rough rocky path) heading across the southern 'shoulder' of Simon Fell, with the broad valley of Fell Beck falling away to your right, for 0.75 miles to reach a ladder stile over a wall (Pen-y-ghent ahead). Cross the stile and continue on along the path gradually dropping down to join a wall on your left after about 0.5 miles, which you follow bending to the left then straight on down to reach a ruined shooters' hut where you follow the path curving to the right to reach a ladder stile beside a gate just beyond a ford.

6. Cross the stile, then continue on along the clear path with the stream and wall just to your left, bearing left at the fork in the path

(stream disappears down Nick Pot) down to join the wall on your left, where the path levels out and becomes grassy underfoot. Carry straight on alongside the wall on your left across limestone pavements to quickly reach a stile over a wall (National Nature Reserve). Cross the stile (wall bends away to the left) and head straight on along the clear path across limestone moorland then, after just over 0.25 miles, the path drops down a small limestone ridge to reach a crossroads of clear grassy tracks (SP).

7. Turn right (SP 'Clapham') and follow the grassy track straight on, with the low limestone ridge on your right, to reach a ladder stile beside a gate across your path (Sulber Gate). Head through the gate and follow the track straight on alongside the wall on your left then, where this wall bends away after 0.25 miles, carry straight on along the track heading across the flat shelf of land for a further 0.25 miles until you reach a fork in the track. Follow the right-hand grassy track bearing gently to the right across the limestone moorland for almost 0.25 miles to reach a fork in the track just after a line of low limestone crags on your right. Head straight on along the left-hand track (leaving the other track to bend away to the right alongside the low crags) then, after a short distance, the track forks again - follow the grassy path bearing up to the right towards the cairn on top of the low hill ahead. Follow the path heading over this hill, passing to the left of this cairn, down to join a rough track which you follow to the left down to reach a gate / ladder stile. Head through the gate and follow the track bearing left down across the hillside to reach a gate in the wall on your left at the top of Long Lane (track).

8. Head through this gate and follow the clear track dropping quite steeply down at first then levelling out (Clapdale to your right) to reach a gate across the track after 0.5 miles (track now enclosed by walls on either side). Carry straight on along the track heading gradually down for a further 0.75 miles before the track drops down into a 'dip' then climbs up to reach a sharp right-hand bend (ignore track to the left). Follow the track to the right (SP 'Clapham') down through tunnels then bending left and round to the right to reach a lane beside Clapham Church. Turn left back into Clapham.

Clapham Walking Weekend
- Sunday Walk -
Clapham, Thwaite Lane, the Norber Erratics & Austwick.

Highlights	Old walled tracks, superb limestone scars, strange alien rocks, the delightful village of Austwick, the legend of the cuckoo and ancient ploughing terraces.
Distance	4.5 miles Time 2.5 hours
Maps	OS Explorer OL2
Refreshments	New Inn and tea rooms at Clapham; Game Cock Inn and shop at Austwick.
Terrain	Clear stony tracks and field paths lead to Austwick. The path below Robin Proctor's Scar is rough underfoot with a short but fairly steep climb up onto the scar, whilst there are steep drops to the side of the path below Nappa Scar. From Austwick, clear field paths lead back to Clapham.
Ascents	Robin Proctor's Scar - 260 metres above sea level
Caution	There are steep drops to the side of the path beneath Nappa Scar. Limestone is slippery when wet.

POINTS OF INTEREST

A track leaves Clapham skirting around the churchyard before climbing up through two tunnels. This is Thwaite Lane, an old walled track that was once a busy route through this area. When the Farrer family built Ingleborough Hall during the 19th Century, they landscaped the land between their new house and the church to create a garden and also built two tunnels to keep the ancient Right of Way from Clapham to Wharfe open, although many believe it was to give themselves some privacy in their new garden from the prying eyes of passers-by along this old lane!

From Thwaite Lane, a path leads off to reach the foot of the impressive limestone screes of Robin Proctor's Scar caused by the North Craven Fault. The scar is said to be named after a local farmer who fell to his death from these limestone cliffs whilst out riding his horse. The famous Norber Erratics can be found on the limestone plateau above these scars. Literally hundreds of large Silurian slate boulders were carried here by a glacier during the last Ice Age some 10,000 years ago from the western slopes of Crummackdale. Over the centuries, the surrounding limestone bedrock has slowly eroded away leaving the more resistant (and darker) slate boulders perched on thin limestone pedestals. Known to geologists and geography students nationwide, these are classic examples of glacial erratics.

Austwick was first settled by Vikings, its name means 'eastern settlement' as at that time the main village in the area was Clapham. There has been friendly rivalry between these two villages for many centuries, so much so that they often have a 'dig' at each other, although usually at the expense of the residents of Austwick. One of the most famous stories relates to the Austwick Cuckoo. The villagers noticed that the arrival of the cuckoo in spring heralded warmer weather and decided to capture one of the birds, and so capture the sunny weather! They found a cuckoo roosting in a nearby tree and built a wall around it during the night, only for the bird to fly away in the morning! Austwick is a delightful village, with a near-perfect scene of old stone cottages facing across a small green complete with an old 'Yorkshire West Riding' signpost and the remains of the market cross. It retains a village atmosphere with shop, pub, hotel and school. Of particular note is Austwick Hall, a fine house dating back to at least the early 16th Century originally built as a fortified manor house. To the west of the village are ancient ploughing terraces known as lynchets, flat terraces cut into the hillside wide enough for oxen to pull a plough; these terraces allowed crops to be grown on the otherwise steep valley sides. Some may date back to the early Anglo-Saxon farmers who settled in this area, although most are medieval.

Clapham

CLAPHAM SUNDAY WALK

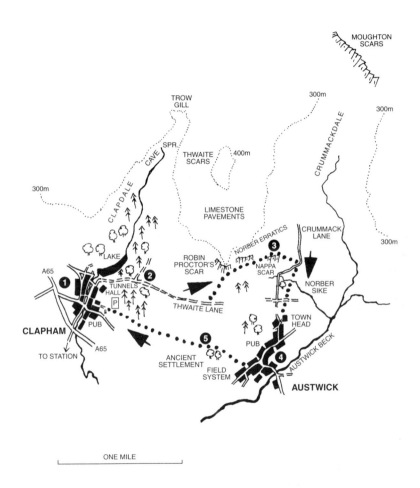

MOUGHTON SCARS

TROW GILL

300m

CLAPDALE

CAVE

SPR.

THWAITE SCARS

400m

CRUMMACKDALE

300m

300m

LIMESTONE PAVEMENTS

300m

NORBER ERRATICS

CRUMMACK LANE

❸

ROBIN PROCTOR'S SCAR

NAPPA SCAR

LAKE

A65

❶

❷

TUNNELS
HALL
P

THWAITE LANE

NORBER SIKE

CLAPHAM

PUB

TO STATION

A65

ANCIENT SETTLEMENT

❺

FIELD SYSTEM

PUB

TOWN HEAD

AUSTWICK BECK

❹

AUSTWICK

ONE MILE

55

THE WALK

1. From the main car park at Clapham, turn right along the road heading up through the village and follow this lane up (Gildersbank) then, as you approach St James Church, turn right along a stony track passing the Clapham Millennium Stone. Follow this track up then almost immediately head to the left just before the stone arch (SP 'Austwick') and follow this clear stony track up through two tunnels. After you have emerged from the tunnels, continue along the clear stony track climbing up then levelling out for a while before the track bends sharp left and forks - follow the right-hand walled track (SP 'Austwick').

2. Follow this very clear stony track straight on then, after just over 0.5 miles where the track drops down slightly, turn left over a ladder stile (SP 'Norber'). Follow the clear grassy path bearing slightly to the right across the field to join a wall corner just below Robin Proctor's Scar then follow this wall round to the right to reach a ladder stile in the corner of the field directly below the Scar. Cross this stile then head straight on alongside the wall on your right (limestone scar on your left) then, where the wall bends away to your right, carry straight on up a small bank (Scar and scree slopes to your left) to reach a junction of paths (SP 'Crummack'). Carry straight on along the clear path bearing slightly to the right down across the rough hillside to join the wall on your right again, which you follow up a short but steep rocky path onto the top of the limestone scar (Norber Erratics to your left), at the top of which carry on for a few paces then turn right over a stone wall stile.

3. After the wall stile, follow the clear path straight on and over another wall stile just below the wooded limestone scar of Nappa Scars, after which follow the clear path along the base of the scar (take care) then along the top of a ridge (with the wall on your left) down to reach a ladder stile at the end of the field that leads onto Crummack Lane. At the lane, cross the stile directly opposite then turn right down across the field, over Norber Sike (stream) and on

to reach a ladder stile to the right of a barn. Cross the stile then head straight on alongside the wall on your left to reach a wall stile in the corner of the field that leads onto an enclosed track. Cross the wall stile directly opposite then head straight on alongside the wall on your left to reach another wall stile at the end of the field that leads into the yard of Town Head Farm on the outskirts of Austwick. Head straight on through the yard, through a bridlegate to the left of the garage then down the clear path to join the road. Turn left along the road down to reach the main road where you turn right into the centre of the village.

4. Follow the road through the village passing the Game Cock Inn then, at the village green (with the stepped cross) follow the road round to the right towards 'Clapham'. Follow this road down through the village then, after approx. 300 yards, cross the stile to the right beside a gate (SP 'Clapham'). Head straight up the hillside bearing very slightly to the right up towards the top of the field up onto a level ploughing terrace (ancient field system) and follow this straight on (wall just up to your right) to reach a wall-gate across your path. After the wall-gate, follow the path bearing to the right across the field across more ploughing terraces (passing a bench), over a wall-stile then straight on passing to the right-side of a small copse of trees, with the wall just to your right, to reach a small wall-gate / stile at the end of the field.

5. Cross this stile then follow the clear path straight on over another stile and down to reach a stile beside a gate (path becomes a grassy track). Follow this grassy track straight on over another stile beside a gate then on to reach a kissing gate at the bottom end of Thwaite Top Plantation. Carry straight on along the clear path, through another kissing gate then on along a fence on your left to reach a wide farm track. Head straight along the farm track (follow the path which runs parallel to the track on the right-hand side) into the farmyard where you follow the lane to the right (SP) again following the path which runs parallel to the track straight on back into Clapham.

COWGILL
Dentdale

*Dentdale is where the Yorkshire Dales meet the Lake District,
a landscape of classic Dales scenery with soaring fells and deep
valleys but the architecture is reminiscent of Lakeland, which gives this
valley a unique feel. This secluded and unfrequented valley was
originally settled by Viking farmers in the 10th Century, their system
of farming and settlement pattern remains largely intact to this day
as many of the farmhouses have Old Norse names and are built as
traditional 'long-houses'. Cowgill, at the head of the valley, is a
dispersed community of farms, a small chapel, Youth Hostel and the
Sportsman's Inn. The valley is steep and narrow with the delightful
River Dee playfully cascading over shelves of limestone and narrow
channels, occasionally disappearing only to re-emerge a few yards
further on, all of which can be seen from the winding valley road
which runs alongside the river.*

THE VILLAGE

Cowgill is a small hamlet tucked away amongst the high fells of Upper Dentdale in the shadow of Whernside. Nevertheless, it boasts a train station (the highest in the country), Youth Hostel, B&B, campsite and the Sportsman's Inn.

ACCOMMODATION

Tourist Information Centre, Sedbergh: 015396 20125

COWGILL PUB

Sportsman's Inn, Cowgill: 015396 25282
Dating back some 300 years, this remote whitewashed old drovers' inn retains many original features including low beamed ceilings and a Dent Marble fireplace. The Dales Way passes its door, although only the foolish would do so.

PUBS ON THE WALKS

Station Inn, Ribblehead: 01524 241274

Cowgill Walking Weekend
- Saturday Walk -
Upper Dentdale, Blea Moor Tunnel, Whernside
& Ribblehead Viaduct

WALK INFORMATION

Highlights   Beautiful Upper Dentdale, wild moorland, Blea Moor Tunnel, the summit of Whernside, incredible views and the magnificent Ribblehead Viaduct.

Distance   10.5 miles (*short route:* 6.5 miles)

Time   5 hours

Maps   OS Explorer Map OL2

Refreshments   Sportsman's Inn at Cowgill or the Station Inn at Ribblehead.

Terrain   After an initial stretch of road walking along a quiet lane, a path leads off past Dent Head Farm to reach the northern entrance of Blea Moor Tunnel. A steep climb then ensues through a plantation (boggy) up onto Blea Moor (following the line of the Tunnel) over to reach Force Gill Aqueduct near the southern entrance of the Tunnel. The ascent from Force Gill up onto the summit of Whernside is long and unremitting, following a stone-flagged path most of the way. The final climb up onto the summit ridge is steep, with steep drops down towards Greensett Tarn. The summit ridge is exposed to the elements. The descent initially heads along the gently falling ridge before a very steep stone-pitched path heads down towards Bruntscar Farm. From Bruntscar, grassy bridleways and stony tracks lead past old farmhouses and then beneath Ribblehead Viaduct to the Station Inn.

Ascents: Blea Moor - 500 metres above sea level
             Whernside - 736 metres above sea level

Caution   This is a strenuous walk to the summit of Whernside with steep paths in places - do not attempt this walk in bad weather. Take a compass and OS map with you. This walk fords a number of streams, which may be difficult after heavy rain.

Linear Walk This is a linear walk from the Sportsman's Inn at Cowgill to Ribblehead Station, from where you catch the train back to Dent Station. It is a 10-minute train ride to Dent Station. Check train times before setting out - call 08457 484950.

Dent Head Viaduct

The finest stretch of the Settle and Carlisle Railway is between the three stations at Garsdale Head, Dent and Ribblehead. From Dent Station, the highest mainline station in England, the railway traces a high-level route across the flanks of Great Knoutberry Hill crossing the impressive Artengill Viaduct and then Dent Head Viaduct before entering the depths of the 2,269-yard long Blea Moor Tunnel. This is undoubtedly one of the greatest railway journeys in the world with superlative views, deep tunnels, tumbling waterfalls, viaducts, ravines and soaring fells all around. Emerging from the tunnel, the railway passes beneath Force Gill Aqueduct, where Victorian engineers skilfully diverted a stream across the line, then on to reach Ribblehead Viaduct, which spans an area of peat bog and wilderness slap bang in the middle of some of the most spectacular scenery in the Yorkshire Dales with Ingleborough and Whernside towering above. Completed in 1876, the Settle to Carlisle Railway was built by the Midland Railway Co. who needed a route to Scotland to compete with the rival coastal lines. It took six years and 6,000 navvies to build the 72 mile line traversing some of the most inhospitable terrain in the country, with 20 viaducts and 14 tunnels. This railway stands as one of the great feats of Victorian engineering - and all built using little more than muscle power. It is only when you see the railway at close hand that you get an idea of what those navvies faced.

From the Sportman's Inn, we follow the quiet narrow lane heading into the upper reaches of Dentdale alongside the playful River Dee. After a while, a path turns off climbing up past Dent Head Farm in the shadow of Dent Head Viaduct over Blea Moor following the line of the tunnel some 500-ft below your feet with a series of air shafts and spoil heaps guiding your way. The views during the decent from Blea Moor towards Force Gill Aqueduct are superb with the distinctive profiles of Ingleborough and Whernside dominating the scene. Force Gill is well named indeed for these words are derived from Old Norse meaning 'waterfall' and 'steep-sided ravine'. A well-trodden path turns off at this

Aqueduct, climbing steadily up through a vast landscape heading for the summit ridge. The views are unrivalled, with Greensett Tarn cradled beneath the summit ridge and falling screes and vast landscapes of peat bogs and limestone moorland all around. But the real highlight is the summit ridge. Many people claim Ingleborough to be the finest mountain in the Dales with views far superior to those from Whernside or Pen-y-Ghent. I would disagree. As you reach the wall that traces across the summit, a view unfolds of the deep and lush valleys of Deepdale and Dentdale snaking away into the distance set beneath the rounded hills of the Howgill Fells. On the horizon, the Lakeland Fells rise and fall whilst to the south-west are the glistening waters of Morecambe Bay. To the north and east are the high fells of the Yorkshire Dales including Mallerstang Edge, Great Shunner Fell, Great Knoutberry Hill, Pen-y-Ghent and the unmistakable outline of Ingleborough.

A very steep path leads down from the summit ridge to join an old track near Bruntscar. This is Kirkby Gate, the old packhorse route to Kirkby Lonsdale that is now a pleasant grassy track for most of the way passing old farmhouses. Our route then heads beneath the Ribblehead Viaduct, with 24 arches soaring 160-ft above your head! Built in 1875, this viaduct still carries the Settle and Carlisle Railway for an amazing quarter of a mile across Batty Moss Moor. The boggy moorland beneath the viaduct was once home to thousands of navvies and their families who lived in the most appalling conditions in shanty towns whilst construction of the viaduct took place. Disease was commonplace and well over 100 men died building Ribblehead Viaduct, many of them buried in unmarked graves across the moor.

COWGILL SATURDAY WALK

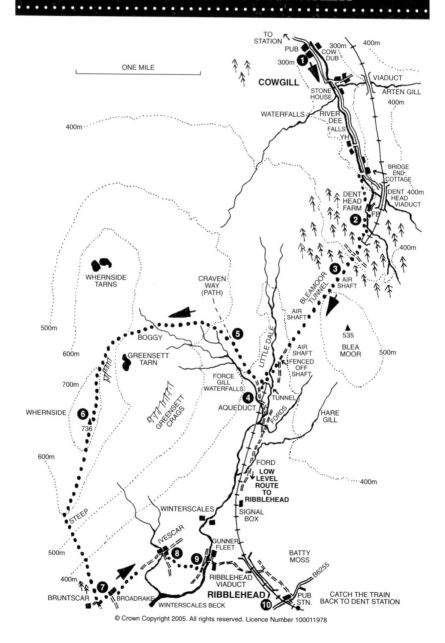

ONE MILE

TO STATION

PUB
300m

COW DUB
300m

1

COWGILL

300m

400m

VIADUCT

STONE HOUSE

ARTEN GILL

400m

WATERFALLS

RIVER DEE

FALLS

YH

400m

BRIDGE END COTTAGE

DENT HEAD FARM

DENT HEAD VIADUCT

DENT 400m HEAD

FB

2

400m

3

AIR SHAFT

WHERNSIDE TARNS

CRAVEN WAY (PATH)

BLEAMOOR TUNNEL

500m

AIR SHAFT

BOGGY

5

LITTLE DALE

AIR SHAFT

535

BLEA MOOR

500m

600m

GREENSETT TARN

700m

FORCE GILL WATERFALLS

AIR SHAFT
FENCED OFF SHAFT

WHERNSIDE

6

736

GREENSETT CRAGS

AQUEDUCT

4

TUNNEL

FORDS

HARE GILL

600m

FORD

LOW LEVEL ROUTE TO RIBBLEHEAD

400m

WINTERSCALES

SIGNAL BOX

STEEP

IVESCAR

GUNNER FLEET

BATTY MOSS

500m

8

9

400m

7

BRUNTSCAR

BROADRAKE

WINTERSCALES BECK

RIBBLEHEAD VIADUCT

RIBBLEHEAD

10

PUB STN.

B6255

CATCH THE TRAIN BACK TO DENT STATION

1. From the Sportsman's Inn at Cowgill (with your back to the pub) turn right along the road and follow this quiet country lane up with the River Dee on your left to soon reach a narrow road bridge (Stone House Bridge). Cross this bridge then follow the road bending round to the right with the river now on your right (Artengill Viaduct above) and follow this road heading up the valley passing the Youth Hostel across the river after just over 0.5 miles. Continue straight on up along the road for a further 0.25 miles to reach an old grass-covered stone bridge to your right across the river opposite the whitewashed Bridge End Cottage (just before the road bends up to the left towards Dent Head Viaduct). Cross the old bridge and head through the gate after which turn left (SP 'Blea Moor') up along the fence with the stream down to your left then, after a short distance, follow the path round to the left over a small FB across the stream and over a stile. After the stile, follow the clear path up alongside the fence on your left - the path soon levels out then leaves the fence behind (by the telegraph pole) and heads straight on bearing very slightly to the right across the boggy rough field to reach Dent Head Farm.

2. Cross the bridge then head to the right passing in front of the farm house to reach a gate at the end of the farmyard. Head straight on along the clear grassy path down to reach a FB across the stream to your right, after which turn left up alongside the stream (spoil heaps on your right) and through a large gap in a wall across your path then on to join a wall on your left by a tunnel beneath the railway embankment. Head up the steep grassy bank keeping close to the wall on your left (railway line down to your left) then keep climbing up passing the entrance to Blea Moor Tunnel. The path levels out and leads over a stile across a fence on the edge of the coniferous forest. After the stile, follow the clear boggy path to the left into the forest and follow the raised grassy track (following the line of the tunnel below ground) through a narrow 'fire break' in the forest then climbing up some steps to reach a clear track across your path. Head

straight over the track along the path ahead and follow it climbing steeply up through a 'fire break' to reach a stile over a fence at the top of the forest.

3. Cross the stile and follow the rough grassy path climbing up passing the Air Shaft then continue straight on along the rough boggy path heading up across Blea Moor to reach a stile over a fence at the top of the moorland. After the stile, carry straight on along the clear grassy path gradually dropping down passing two more Air Shafts (and large spoil heaps) down to reach another large spoil heap and 'hidden shaft' surrounded by high metal fencing. Immediately after passing this fenced-off shaft, where the clear grassy track gently curves away to the left, branch off to the right straight on alongside the large spoil heap on your right (no clear path) and down across Little Dale Beck, after which head on alongside the stream on your left for a short distance then climb up the low grassy bank to your right. At the top of the grassy bank, continue straight on across rough boggy moorland to soon reach the stone wall above the southern entrance to Blea Moor Tunnel. Follow this wall up to the right to reach a stile over a fence (just above where the wall bends to the left), then head straight on alongside the wall on your left and down to reach a clear path beside Force Gill Aqueduct / bridge above the railway line.

(*Short route to Ribblehead Station: Follow the clear path to the left over the bridge above the railway line beside Force Gill Aqueduct then curving round to the right (with Force Gill on your right) and follow this clear wide track (railway across to your right) all the way to reach Blea Moor Signal Box after 0.75 miles. Continue straight on along the track alongside the railway then down to join the clear stony track in the shadow of Ribblehead Viaduct which you follow straight on up to reach the road beside the Station Inn at Ribblehead. The entrance to the station is opposite the pub.*)

4. As you reach this clear path beside Force Gill Aqueduct, turn right back on yourself (away from Force Gill Aqueduct) along the clear

path (SP 'Dentdale') and follow this climbing straight up the hillside, with Force Gill and waterfall across to your left, along a stone-pitched path to reach a bridle-gate in a fence. After the bridle-gate, continue straight on along a clear stony path climbing steadily up the rough hillside with Force Gill across to your left then, halfway up this hillside, cross the stile to the left over the fence (SP 'Whernside').

5. Follow the clear path on across grassy moorland, level at first then gently bearing up to the left to join a wall on your right. Follow the path up alongside this wall gradually climbing up (with some flat sections) then, as you approach the bottom of the steep summit ridge of Whernside, the path bears to the left away from the wall across boggy ground. Follow the stone-flagged path gradually rising up (with Greensett Tarn just across to your left) before a final steep climb up to re-join the wall-line on the 'shoulder' of the summit ridge of Whernside. As you join the wall, follow the path to the left alongside this wall and follow it climbing gradually up then along the flat summit ridge to reach the windbreak on the summit of Whernside.

6. Continue straight on along the clear path alongside the wall gradually dropping down to reach a bridle-gate across your path. Head through the bridle-gate and continue straight on gradually dropping down across the ridge then down two short but steep rocky limestone 'steps' along the ridge, at the bottom of which follow the clear path to the left heading away from the wall. Follow this pitched-stone path dropping very steeply down the flanks of Whernside to reach a wall-gate across your path. After the wall-gate, continue straight on down over a ladder stile beside a gate then continue on down to reach another gate beside a stone barn (near the farm buildings of Bruntscar).

7. Head through the gate and turn left immediately after the barn (SP 'Winterscales'). Follow the clear path across pastureland to join a track at Broadrake Farm which you follow straight on passing in front of the farmhouse then on passing to the right of the barn

heading across the field to reach a bridle-gate in a wall across your path. Continue straight on along the clear path across fields through a succession of bridle-gates to join a rough grassy track that leads on to reach Ivescar Farm.

8. Head through the gate into the farmyard passing in front of the farmhouse and over a bridge immediately after which follow the farm lane to the right then, just after leaving the farmyard (and the stone barn on your left), head left over a stile beside a gate. After the stile, head to the right across the field to a wall stile in the corner of the field, after which head straight on with the wall on your left up over a small hill and down over a stile in a fence then continue on alongside the wall on your left for a short distance to reach a ladder stile in a corner of this field (where the wall bends to the right). Cross the ladder stile, then head to the right across the rough field to a ladder stile just beyond a telegraph pole, after which head on with the wall on your left to reach a metalled farm lane.

9. Turn left along the lane towards Gunnerfleet Farm, through a gate across your path then turn right along a track before the large barns over a bridge across Winterscales Beck. Follow this clear stony track winding straight on to pass beneath Ribblehead Viaduct, after which follow it round to the right to reach the road beside the Station Inn at Ribblehead. The entrance to Ribblehead Station is opposite the pub.

10. *Catch the train from Ribblehead Station to Dent Station.* From Dent Station, head along the access lane to quickly reach the road where you turn left and follow it winding steeply down to reach a road junction at the bottom of the hill at Lea Yeat. Turn left over Lea Yeat Bridge (SP 'Newby Head, Hawes, Ingleton') across the River Dee and follow the lane back alongside the river on your left to the Sportsman's Inn.

Cowgill Walking Weekend
- Sunday Walk -
Dent Station, Great Knoutberry Hill
& Artengill Viaduct.

WALK INFORMATION

Highlights — England's highest station, great views from Great Knoutberry, the old road from Scotland and Artengill Viaduct.

Distance	6 miles	Time	3 hours

Maps — OS Explorer OL2

Refreshments — Sportsman's Inn at Cowgill

Terrain — From the Sportsman's Inn, a quiet narrow lane leads through Lea Yeat then climbs steeply up to reach Dent Station. After another stretch of road walking a track leads southwards skirting across the upper flanks of Great Knoutberry Hill to the old Widdale Road (track). This is then followed steeply down passing beneath Artengill Viaduct to re-join the road from where it is a short walk back to the Sportsman's Inn.

Ascents: — (flanks of) Great Knoutberry Hill - 540 metres above sea level

Caution — This walk involves a number of long and quite steep ascents and descents. Some sections of track are rough and boggy underfoot. The flanks of Great Knoutberry Hill are exposed to the elements.

POINTS OF INTEREST

This circular walk takes in Dent Station, the highest mainline station in England that is actually four miles (and 600-ft higher) from the village of Dent! With such an exposed location, the Station Master's house is said to have been the first house in the country fitted with double glazing. The station lies on the world-famous Settle and Carlisle Railway, which was built during the 1870's by the Midland Railway Company. Undeterred by the inhospitable terrain, the Victorian engineers set about designing a route that would eventually create one of the world's greatest railway journeys. From the (relatively) gentle landscape of Ribblehead, the line then had to cross a range of hills before descending into the Eden Valley; this was done via a series of viaducts and tunnels as well as the three famous viaducts of Ribblehead, Dent Head and Artengill. At Artengill the navvies had to dig down over 150-ft through the peat layer before reaching a solid rock base for the arches.

Our walk follows a fine track across the upper slopes of Great Knoutberry Hill, with the railway on the hillside below and magnificent views down the length of the gently curving valley of Dentdale with the massive bulk of Whernside looming above. This track is known as Galloway Gate, an ancient drovers' road that was once used as a main route from Scotland and the North of England for Scottish-bred cattle bound for the markets of Southern England. The track curves round into the steep-sided side valley of Arten Gill where it joins the old road over to Widdale, near to some long disused primitive coal pits known as Cross Pits Colliery. This fine old track is then followed steadily down through Arten Gill passing beneath the impressive 11-arch viaduct to reach the valley floor.

COWGILL SUNDAY WALK

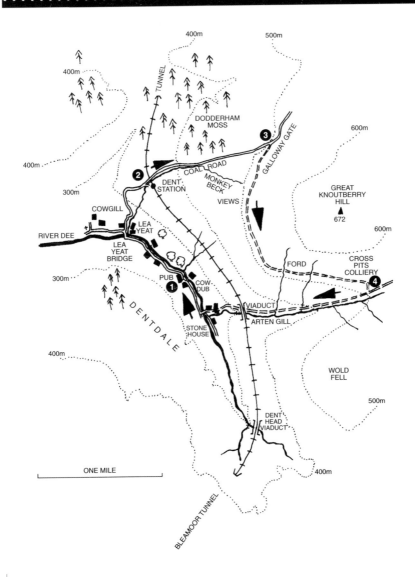

400m
500m

TUNNEL

DODDERHAM
MOSS

400m

GALLOWAY GATE

600m

COAL ROAD

400m

300m

DENT
STATION

MONKEY
BECK

VIEWS

GREAT
KNOUTBERRY
HILL
▲
672

600m

COWGILL

LEA
YEAT

RIVER DEE

LEA
YEAT
BRIDGE

FORD

CROSS
PITS
COLLIERY

300m

PUB

COW
DUB

DENTDALE

STONE
HOUSE

VIADUCT

ARTEN GILL

400m

WOLD
FELL

500m

DENT
HEAD
VIADUCT

ONE MILE

400m

BLEAMOOR TUNNEL

1. From the Sportsman's Inn (with your back to the pub) turn left along the quiet country lane, with the River Dee on your right, for just over 0.5 miles to reach the road-bridge (Lea Yeat Bridge) across the River Dee. Cross the bridge then take the road turning to the right (just after the 'phone box) towards 'Dent Station, Garsdale Head' and follow the road winding very steeply up to reach Dent Station.

2. Continue up along the road (Coal Road) passing the entrance lane to the station, over the bridge across the railway and follow it climbing steadily up passing a large coniferous plantation on your left then, after about a mile from Dent Station, take the stony track to the right through a gate (SP 'Stone House, Widdale') just as the road begins to veer to the left.

3. Follow this clear rough track (Galloway Gate) straight on across the upper flanks of Great Knoutberry Hill, with superb views down into Dentdale to your right. After about a mile the track begins to curves gradually round to the left into the side valley of Arten Gill, although keeping roughly to the same contours of the hillside, then as you near the head of Arten Gill at the top of the 'pass' over into Widdale, follow the track bending sharply down to the right to join a walled track heading up out of Arten Gill.

4. Turn right along this walled track heading steadily down into Arten Gill to reach the impressive Artengill Viaduct which carries the Settle and Carlisle Railway above this ravine. Pass beneath this viaduct and continue down along the clear track to reach a metalled lane at the hamlet of Stone House, and follow this lane straight on to quickly reach the main valley road beside a very narrow stone bridge. Turn right along the road over the narrow bridge and follow this quiet country lane bending to the right after the bridge then straight on, with the River Dee on your right, back to the Sportsman's Inn.

GRASSINGTON

Wharfedale

Grassington is an attractive small town set in the heart of Wharfedale, a popular tourist destination due to its picturesque cobbled square, stone cottages and winding alleyways, known locally as folds. Grassington developed as a trading centre in the Forest of Wharfedale as it lay on two important routes, the monastic road from Fountains Abbey to the Lake District and the road from Skipton to Wensleydale.

The town was granted a market charter in 1282 which secured its status as the 'capital of the upper dale', however, regular markets lapsed in the late 19th Century. The monks of Fountains Abbey also owned grazing lands in the area and brought large flocks of sheep this way en route to their monastic farms throughout the North of England. They had a farm at Grassington known as Hardy Grange (private), which can still be found hidden away along Gills Fold although the present building is largely 17th Century. Grassington's heyday was during the 18th and 19th centuries when the lead mines at Yarnbury on the moors above Grassington were developed by the Dukes of Devonshire. By the early 1900's mining had virtually ended due to cheaper imports and dwindling reserves.

THE VILLAGE

Grassington boasts a good selection of shops including Barclays Bank, outdoor pursuits shop, general stores, Post Office, craft shops, fish & chip shop, restaurants, cafés, bookshop, Off Licence, newsagents, garage, Folk Museum and a good selection of hotels, pubs and B&B's

ACCOMMODATION

National Park Information Centre, Grassington: 01756 751690

GRASSINGTON PUBS

Black Horse Hotel, Grassington: **01756 752770**
This imposing old coaching inn stands just off the cobbled square at the heart of Grassington. The spacious interior is warmed by a log fire set in a large stone fireplace.

Devonshire Hotel, Grassington: **01756 752525**
This lovely stone-built hotel dominates the old cobbled square, named after the Duke of Devonshire who was instrumental in the development of the local lead mines and who still owns large tracts of Wharfedale.

Foresters Arms, Grassington: **01756 752349**
This traditional village pub boasts a lively atmosphere as well as an excellent range of well-kept Real Ales.

Grassington House Hotel: **01756 752406**
The cosy Real Ale bar forms part of this large hotel. Inside, open fires warm the bar whilst there is also a conservatory for summer evenings.

PUBS ALONG THE WALKS

Fountaine Inn, Linton: 01756 752210
Red Lion, Burnsall   01756 720204
Clarendon Hotel, Hebden   01756 752446

Grassington Walking Weekend
- Saturday Walk -

Grassington, Linton, Thorpe, Burnsall
& the River Wharfe

WALK INFORMATION

Highlights   Powerful Linton Falls, Vanbrugh's almshouses, the hidden village, Yorkshire's Dick Whittington, by the banks of the Wharfe and the murder of Dr Petty.

Distance   8 miles   Time   4 hours

Maps   OS Explorer OL2

Refreshments   Pubs at Grassington, Linton and Burnsall. Shops and tea rooms at Grassington and Burnsall.

Terrain   From Grassington, a footbridge crosses above Linton Falls before a quiet lane leads up into Linton, from where a mixture of tracks, field paths and quiet lanes lead up across the lower slopes of Burnsall & Thorpe Fell skirting behind Elbolton Hill into Thorpe. A clear path then leads across a succession of fields through squeeze-stiles to Burnsall. A clear riverside path leads upstream all the way back to Grassington.

Ascents: Elbolton Hill - 290 metres above sea level

Caution   Take care when crossing the B6160 near Linton. This walk crosses limestone terrain - limestone is slippery when wet. Take care along the banks of the Wharfe particularly after heavy rain, and keep well away from the edge of Loop Scar.

From Grassington, a walled path leads down across a footbridge above Linton Falls where the River Wharfe tumbles over rocks caused by the Craven Fault, an impressive sight after heavy rain. Note the weir and old mill race which once provided power for Linton Mill before it closed in 1959. A mill has stood on this site since medieval times, however, the old mill buildings were demolished and new houses built in the 1980's, although some millworkers' cottages remain. Linton Church, dedicated to St Michael and All Angels, has a lovely setting beside the Wharfe and dates from Norman times, although much altered in the 14th and 15th centuries. It is built in characteristic Dales' style and still serves the surrounding villages. Linton-in-Craven is one of the prettiest villages in the Dales with old cottages facing across a tree-shaded green. At one end of the green stands the Fountaine Hospital, a fine Georgian building reputedly designed by Vanbrugh. The Hospital incorporates six almshouses and a chapel and was endowed by Richard Fountaine in 1721 for six poor of the parish. Richard Fountaine made his fortune as a timber merchant and coffin maker in London during the Plague of 1665 and the Great Fire of 1666 and became an Alderman of the City.

A path leads up from Linton skirting behind Elbolton Hill beneath the gritstone outcrops of Burnsall & Thorpe Fell then down through the 'secret valley' to reach the hidden village of Thorpe, which lies between the twin limestone hills of Elbolton and Kail. During the Border quarrels of the Middle Ages, local people would seek refuge from Scottish raiders in this village. Burnsall is an attractive village with a large green beside the River Wharfe surrounded by old stone cottages and a fine Dales' inn. St Wilfrid's Church dates back to pre-Conquest days, as the many ancient cross fragments inside the church testify. Beside the church is the village school, a lovely old building that was founded as a Grammar School in 1602 by William Craven, Yorkshire's very own Dick Whittington who set out from the neighbouring village of Appletreewick to travel to London to seek his fortune. This he found, and he rose to become Lord Mayor of London, but he never forgot his roots and gave generously to many local projects. From Burnsall, a delightful riverside path leads up passing the limestone gorge of Loup Scar all the way back to Grassington, with a swaying bridge thrown in for good measure. The rapids of Loup Scar hold a dark secret. Back in the 18th Century, Tom Lee was the blacksmith at Grassington but also a notorious robber. Dr Petty knew as much and threatened to tell the authorities, however, after an evening at a hostelry at Kilnsey, Lee murdered Dr Petty on his way home through Grass Wood and threw his body into the river at Loup Scar. He was only caught after his servant broke down and confessed, and Lee was sentenced to death.

Grassington

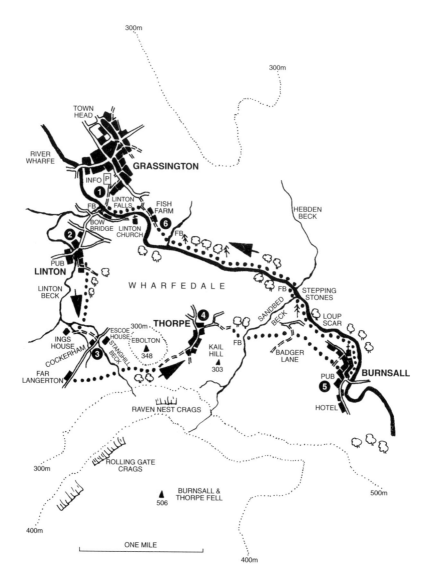

THE WALK

1. With your back to the Yorkshire Dales National Park Centre at Grassington, head to the left across the parking area to a wall-gate in the bottom left corner of the field that leads onto an enclosed path which you follow down to reach the FB across the River Wharfe (Linton Falls). After the FB, follow the path to the right skirting around the houses (ignore the packhorse bridge) to reach the road (detour along the road to the left to Linton Church). Turn right along the road up to a T-junction where you head straight on up to reach a crossroads then continue straight on along the lane into Linton.

2. As you reach the road-bridge across Linton Beck in the centre of the village, turn left along the lane with the stream on your right (passing the packhorse bridge and ford) and follow this on to quickly reach the entrance to Grange Farm at the edge of the village. Turn left at the farm entrance through a bridle-gate (SP 'Thorpe Lane, Threapland') and follow the fence on your right skirting around the farm to reach a bridle-gate (SP), after which head up alongside the wall on your right and through another bridle-gate to the right that leads onto a farm track. Turn left along the track then, after a few paces, turn right along a level grassy track (SP 'Threapland') and follow this straight on across the field to reach a gate across your path. Just after this gate the track forks - follow the right-hand track down to quickly reach a wall-gate beside a gate (at the end of the clear track). Head through the gate and walk straight on alongside the wall on your left to reach a wall-stile at the end of the field, after which continue straight on across two more fields and over a wall-stile to the right of a stone barn that leads onto a stony track. Turn left up along the track to reach the road.

3. Turn right up along the road for 0.5 miles to reach Far Langerton Farm where you turn left over a ladder stile beside a gate (SP

'Thorpe'). Head left across the field over another ladder stile, after which continue straight on bearing very slightly to the right across the hillside over four wall-stiles then out onto a larger field where you continue on bearing slightly to the right down through a gate / ford across Stanghill Beck after which carry straight on alongside the fence on your right to reach a ladder stile in the top right corner of the field (at the foot of Elbolton Hill). After the ladder stile, follow the grassy track to the right through two old stone gateposts after which follow the grassy path straight on gently curving to the left around the foot of Elbolton Hill to join a wall on your right - the path now becomes a clear grassy track that drops down to reach a gate at the top of a walled track, which you follow into Thorpe. The walled track joins a metalled lane at the top of the village, which you follow to the left to reach a road junction in the centre of the village beside the triangular village green.

4. At the road-junction, turn right passing The Manor House on your left and follow the lane up out of the village then, where the lane bends round to the left, take the track to the right through a gate (SP 'Burnsall'). Follow this walled track straight on then bending down to the left to reach a small wall-gate to the right just before the gate at the end of the track. After the wall-gate, head down to the right to reach a bridle-gate at the bottom of the field, after which head on alongside the wall on your left down to reach a small FB across Sandbed Beck. After the stream, head up the bank then follow the clear path straight on across fields through two squeeze-stiles then along a level grassy path to reach the walled track of Badger Lane. Cross the wall-stile opposite (SP 'Burnsall) and head up across the field bearing very slightly to the right then straight on across the middle of the field (Burnsall comes into view) before dropping down to reach a wall-stile at the bottom of the field, after which head right across the next field to reach a wall-stile in the far right-hand corner. A clear path now leads straight on across narrow fields over ten wall-stiles to eventually reach a passageway between the houses that leads onto the road at Burnsall.

5. Turn right along the road and follow it to reach the road junction outside the Red Lion, where you head straight on towards Burnsall Bridge, however, follow the path to the left-side of the bridge (SP 'Dales Way, Hebden Suspension Bridge') to quickly join the riverbank. Follow this riverside path to the left heading upstream (with the Wharfe on your right) out of Burnsall then continue on to reach the limestone gorge of Loup Scar. The path rises up above this gorge then drops back down to river level and follows the wooded riverbank all the way to the Suspension Bridge. Cross the Suspension Bridge then turn immediately left through a bridle-gate. Head straight on along the clear riverside path, with the river now on your left, heading up through the narrow yet shallow river valley, to reach some woodland after about 0.75 miles. Carry straight on through a series of bridle-gates to soon emerge from the woodland, at which point the narrow river valley opens out onto a broader field - follow the path bearing slightly to the right away from the river over a FB across a side-stream then on over a farm track to quickly reach a gate in a wall that leads onto a track.

6. Head up along the track, which soon becomes a metalled lane that leads straight on between some houses then bends round to the left at a fish farm then, where the lane bends sharply to the right, cross the wall-stile to the left (SP 'Grassington, Linton Falls'). Head straight across the field to join a fence above the steep riverbank - follow this fence straight on down a bank then across fields over wall-stiles to join a walled path beside the FB above Linton Falls. Turn right up along the walled path back into Grassington.

Grassington Walking Weekend
- Sunday Walk -
Grassington, Hebden Gill, Yarnbury Lead Mines & Lea Green

WALK INFORMATION

Highlights	Old lanes and traditional meadows, a lead mining village, dramatic Hebden Gill, the desolate landscape of Yarnbury and England's largest Iron Age settlement.
Distance	7 miles Time 3 hours
Maps	OS Explorer OL2
Refreshments	Pubs at Grassington and Hebden. Shops and tea rooms at Grassington and Hebden.
Terrain	Old stony / grassy tracks and field paths lead from Grassington to Hebden, from where an old miners' track leads steadily up through Hebden Gill alongside the tumbling Hebden Beck to reach Yarnbury with its extensive lead mining remains. From Yarnbury a walled track heads across grassy moorland before a clear but narrow path gradually drops back down to Grassington across Lea Green (prehistoric settlement).
Ascents	New Pasture Edge (near Yarnbury) - 399 metres above sea level.
Caution	This walk heads through the old lead mining area of Yarnbury, with crumbling buildings and old mine shafts and levels - do not explore the old workings and keep to the track. The track fords Hebden Beck three times, which may be difficult after heavy rain.

This walk explores the rich archaeological remains that lie scattered across the wild moorland above Grassington. From Hebden, an old track leads steadily up through the steep-sided valley of Hebden Gill to reach the scarred landscape around Yarnbury. This area is littered with the fascinating remains of the lead mining industry that flourished during the 18th and 19th Centuries, developed by the Dukes of Devonshire who owned the land and mines. The earliest shafts were bell pits dating mainly from the 17th Century, however, as technology improved during the late 18th Century deeper shafts, furnaces, drainage systems, smelt mills and flue systems were constructed. The Cupola smelt mill chimney stands 60-feet high and is an unmistakable landmark for miles around. Information boards and a marked Lead Mining Trail help explain the crumbling ruins. Extreme care must be taken when exploring this area.

From Yarnbury, an old track leads across the moors before a path slants back down towards Grassington across an area known as Lea Green. This is the site of one of the largest Iron Age settlements in England that was occupied from 200BC until 400AD, surviving throughout the Roman occupation because of its secluded location high on the hills. Rectangular fields, hut circles and traces of roads can be clearly seen, although to the untrained eye it appears to be a very rough scattering of fields covered with lots of grassy bumps! As with many other archaeological sites, the true picture only really comes to life when viewed from the air, although its windswept location certainly stirs the imagination. Just before you join the walled track as you approach Grassington, the surrounding fields have much more defined and regular grass-covered earthworks and bumps. This was the site of the original village of Grassington, which was established by Anglo-Saxon settlers in the 7th Century but abandoned in the 12th Century when the Manor was transferred from the Percys of Northumberland to the Plumpton family and the present-day town established just to the east. Indeed, the name of the town is thought to be derived from a Saxon farmer called Garr who settled in this area and cleared an enclosure or 'tun'.

GRASSINGTON SUNDAY WALK

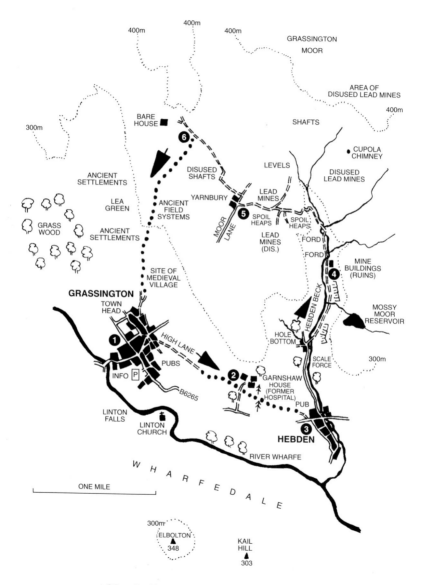

THE WALK

1. From Grassington's cobbled Market Place, walk up along Main Street to reach the small 'square' and crossroads beside the Town Hall where you turn right then, just after the Town Hall, turn left up along Low Lane. Follow this up then, where the lane divides after a short distance (at Garrs End), turn left up along High Lane (SP 'Hebden, Edge Lane) and follow this walled stony track rising up out of the village. The track soon levels out and leads on for a further 0.5 miles to reach a gate at the end of the walled track. Head through the gate and carry on along the track with the wall on your right for a short distance then, where the track and wall bends to the right, head straight on across the field to join a wall corner on your left (SP) then head on alongside this wall to reach a wall-gate beside a gate in the corner of the field (where you re-join the track). Head straight on along the track for a short distance then, where it curves slightly to the right, bear very slightly to the left off the track (SP) heading straight on to reach a wall-stile (just up to the left of the gates across the track) that leads onto a small section of enclosed track. Cross over the track and head through the wall-gate ahead, after which walk straight on across the field keeping close to the wall on your right, over two wall-stiles and into woodland.

2. Follow the clear path straight on through woodland, over a road then straight on across meadows along a clear flagged path (with houses across to your left - site of former Grassington Hospital) then through a small belt of woodland to reach a wall-stile. Cross the wall-stile and head straight on across two fields through small wall-gates then straight down across the narrow field, with the fence / wall on your right, to reach a gate across your path at the bottom of the field at the top of a walled track. Follow this track straight on to join the road on the outskirts of Hebden.

3. Turn left down along the road passing the Clarendon pub on your left immediately after which turn left along a lane (just before the

road-bridge at the bottom of the dip) and follow this straight on with Hebden Beck on your right to reach a gate across the road at the edge of the village (SP 'Yarnbury'). Continue straight on along this lane for a further 0.5 miles gradually climbing up to reach the hamlet of Hole Bottom. At the houses, head straight on along the lane down to quickly reach a gate across the lane (SP on the gate 'BW to Yarnbury') - ignore the two lanes that branch off to left. Head through the gate and follow the stony track bending round to the right over a bridge across Hebden Beck then continue upstream with Hebden Beck on your left. Follow this track for 0.75 miles through a series of gates gradually rising up to reach a group of derelict mining buildings.

4. Continue straight on passing these buildings and through another gate, after which continue along the track for a short distance then drop down to the left over some stepping stones across the stream. Continue upstream alongside the wall, with the stream on your right, to reach a gate beside a wooden barrier across the stream. Head through the gate and carry straight on with the stream on your right then, at the second ford, follow the track slanting up the hillside to the left across spoil heaps then down to re-join the stream. Continue along the track for a short distance then, just after an old lime-kiln, follow the stony track curving up to the left away from the stream and follow this winding up to join a wall on your right which quickly leads to a gate in a corner of this wall (SP). Head through the gate and follow the stony track gently rising up through an area of spoil heaps (ignore any tracks off this main track), passing through a large gap in a wall then continue on to join a clearer track (Duke's New Road) which you follow straight on bearing to the left passing more workings to reach the road opposite the houses at Yarnbury.

5. Turn right up along the road (rough track) for about 100 yards then take the track to the left (SP 'Conistone'). Follow this clear track straight on for 0.5 miles to reach a gate across your path at the end of the walled track. Head through the gate and continue along the

track across the open grassy moorland leaving the wall to curve gently away to your left then, after about 75 yards, turn left off the track along a narrow grassy path that quickly leads to a ladder stile in a corner of this wall (over the wall that curved away to the left).

6. Cross the stile then follow the grassy path bearing slightly to the right across the rough grassy moorland then gently dropping down over a tumbledown wall / line of old workings to reach a wall-stile. After the wall-stile, head to the left along the clear grassy path to reach a ladder stile over a wall then continue on along the narrow path bearing slightly to the left across the grassy moorland to join a wider grassy track that quickly leads to a small wall-gate - do not continue along the grassy track heading alongside the wall. After the wall-gate, continue on bearing slightly to the left passing a corner of a wall then on down to join another grassy path which you follow down to reach a ladder stile in the bottom corner of the field (SP). Cross the ladder stile and follow the clear grassy path bearing slightly to the left across the field (Lea Green) to a wall-stile, after which carry on bearing to the left across the field, over two tumbledown walls then over a large ladder stile. After the ladder stile, continue on bearing to the left to reach a squeeze stile in a wall after which head on alongside the wall on your left (Grassington ahead) down to join a grassy track which you follow straight on (field becomes narrower) to reach a gate and stile just after a small stream at the bottom of the field. Head through the gate and follow the clear enclosed track bending round to the left (SP 'Grassington') then down to join the road at Town Head where you turn left back into Grassington.

HAWES

Wensleydale

*Hawes lies at the head of Wensleydale, the highest market town
in Yorkshire at 850-ft above sea level cradled by the rounded bulks of
Wether Fell, Great Shunner Fell and Widdale Fell; 'hawes' is derived
from the Old Norse word for a mountain pass. First mentioned in 1307,
it remained little more than a clearing in the forest for many centuries,
however, the increasing packhorse trade along routes that converged at
Hawes meant that the town was granted a market charter in 1699,
taking over from Askrigg as the market for Upper Wensleydale.
The Lancaster to Richmond Turnpike came this way in 1795 and then
the railway arrived in the 1870's, which opened up new markets for
local stone, agricultural and dairy products as well as bringing in tourists.
The railway closed for passengers in 1954 and freight in 1964, although
there are efforts to re-open the line once again. Hawes is a busy small
market town serving the needs of a wide geographical area as well as
catering for the large number of visitors who come to this 'town amongst
the hills' and the many foot-sore walkers tackling the Pennine Way.
Hawes is also famous for its cheese for it is the home of Wensleydale
Creamery, makers of the only real Wensleydale cheese in the world!*

THE VILLAGE

Hawes is a bustling market town with plenty of facilities including pubs, hotels, B&B's, Youth Hostel and campsite. Here you will find a range of traditional shops including a butcher, baker, delicatessen, chemist, general stores, outdoor shops, craft shops as well as restaurants, cafés, fish & chip shop, Dales Countryside Museum, Wensleydale Creamery Visitor Centre, a working ropemakers, HSBC and Barclays banks.

ACCOMMODATION

National Park Information Centre, Hawes: 01969 666210

HAWES PUBS

Fountain Hotel, Hawes: **01969 667206**
This 17th Century coaching inn boasts a comfortable lounge bar, games area and large restaurant. Popular with both locals and visitors.

Board Hotel, Hawes: **01969 667223**
The Board is a great example of a traditional town pub with a cosy lounge bar that is always busy with locals.

The Crown, Hawes: **01969 667212**
Literally next door to the Board Hotel, this market town pub has two separate rooms with open fires and traditional décor.

White Hart Hotel, Hawes: **01969 667259**
The White Hart Inn has changed little since the days when stagecoaches pulled up outside its door en route from Lancaster to Richmond - note the bell high up on the wall that was once used to summon fresh horses from the stables.

PUBS ALONG THE WALKS

Rose & Crown, Bainbridge   01969 650225
Green Dragon, Hardraw   01969 667392
Simonstone Hall Hotel (Game Tavern)   01969 667255

Hawes Walking Weekend
- Saturday Walk -
Hawes, Crag Hill, Raydale, Semerwater & Bainbridge

WALK INFORMATION

Highlights	Windswept Wether Fell, Roman roads and fort, a high-level ridge walk, hidden Raydale with its glacial lake, England's shortest river and the 'old road' through Wensleydale.
Distance	12 miles **Time** 6 hours
Maps	OS Explorer OL30
Refreshments	Pubs, tea rooms and shops at Hawes and Bainbridge.
Terrain	The climb from Burtersett across the flanks of Yorburgh and Wether Fell to reach Cam High Road (Roman Road) follows a steep stony track. A clear grassy track / path then heads across the wide ridge of Crag Hill, with views across Raydale, before a steep descent down to reach the road at Countersett. After another short but steep section of road-walking to reach Semerwater Bridge, a riverside path leads to Bainbridge. The return leg follows grassy tracks and field paths along the 'Old Road' through Wensleydale with one or two short sections along quiet lanes.
Ascents	Wether Fell - 530 metres above sea level
Caution	The ascent up onto Wether Fell follows a rough stony track and is steep in places, whilst the descent down across the flanks of Crag Hill follows a steep path. Crag Hill is exposed to the elements.

POINTS OF INTEREST

Wether Fell looms high over the upper reaches of Wensleydale, a huge ridge of moorland that separates Wensleydale from neighbouring Raydale. Wensleydale has its own distinctive character that sets it apart from the other main valleys in the Yorkshire Dales. The wide valley is lush and gentle, the high fells never crowd the river and thriving villages are scattered throughout its length. But climb up across the flanks of Wether Fell and the scene changes quite dramatically as you enter a landscape of windswept moorland, high fells and superb views. A fine ridge walk then ensues across Crag Hill with Raydale falling steeply away to your right and the glacial lake of Semerwater glistening along the valley floor. Semerwater is one of only three large natural sheets of water in Yorkshire, a distinction that has given rise to several legends. Centuries ago, the Devil was stood atop Crag Hill and threw a large boulder in retaliation at a giant who was stood on Addlebrough across the valley. The Devil's Stone can still be seen on the western upper flanks of Addlebrough, whilst the giant's stone fell short and landed on the shores of Semerwater. This stone, known as the Carlow Stone, is actually a glacial erratic - a large boulder of Shap granite brought down by the ice thousands of years ago. Another story tells of how a prosperous city once stood where the lake is now. An angel, dressed as a poor man, tried in vain to find a bed for the night. He eventually found a humble house on a hill away from the city where he was given food and shelter. The next morning he thanked the couple for their hospitality then turned towards the city and cried:

Semerwater rise, Semerwater sink,
And cover all save this li'le house, That gave me meat and drink.

There was a crack of thunder, the heavens opened and the city was engulfed by waves. There may be some truth in this because when the level of the lake was lowered in 1937 evidence of prehistoric pile dwellings were discovered. From Semerwater, we follow a riverside path alongside the Bain, England's shortest river, which drains into the Ure just beyond Bainbridge.

For more information about Bainbridge, please see Walking Weekend 1

HAWES SATURDAY WALK

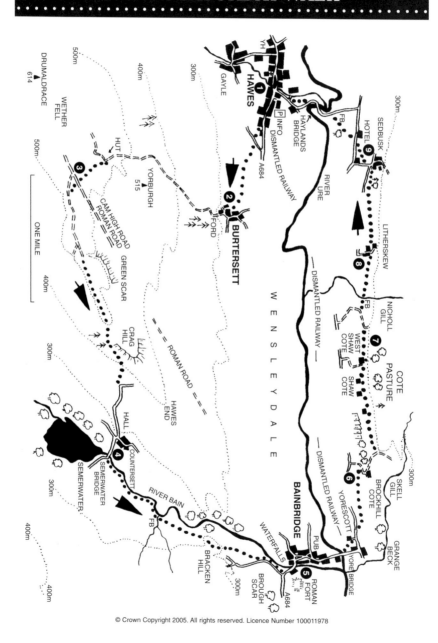

THE WALK

1. From the centre of Hawes, turn left down through the Market Place then, where the road divides at the HSBC bank, follow the one-way system to the left. Follow this road down heading out of the town centre, over a bridge across Gayle Beck then continue straight on along the main A684 road (Burtersett Road) heading out of Hawes. Just before the last houses on your right take the FP to the right through a kissing gate before the 'Wensleydale Press' building (SP 'Burtersett'). Follow the flagged path straight on to quickly reach a lane. Cross the road and take the path opposite to the left (SP 'Burtersett'), and follow the clear path to the left to quickly reach a small wall gate, after which continue along the clear stone-flagged path across several fields through a series of wall gaps. As you approach the houses of Burtersett, the flagged path divides (just before a wall and gate in front of you) - follow the right-hand path that leads uphill and on between the houses into Burtersett.

2. Turn right and follow the road up through the village then, where the road bends round to the left just after the small village 'green', take the lane to the right ('Dead End' sign). Walk along this lane then, almost immediately, take the stony track up to the left (SP 'Wether Fell') and follow this out of Burtersett to reach a gate across your path just after a small ford. Head through the gate and follow the stony track bending steeply up to the right winding up to soon reach a flat shelf of land where you follow the track to the right up to reach a gate in a wall. Head through the gate and follow the clear track climbing steadily up across the flanks of Yorburgh through another gate then, as you approach a wall in front of you, follow the track bending up to the left winding up to reach the top of the 'pass' (with Yorburgh to your left and the crags of Wether Fell across to your right). At the top of the 'pass', the track levels out and becomes a grassy track that leads straight on (ignore the gate and squeeze-stile in the wall to your right) down to a large gap in the wall across your path near to a small hut. Head through the wall-gap and

follow the track for a few paces then take the grassy path that branches very slightly off to the left (leaving the sunken track to bend sharply up to the right) then gently curves very slightly to the right before heading straight on along a clear narrow path down into a shallow 'hollow' then climbing up over a tumbledown wall. After the wall, carry straight on heading over the 'shoulder' of Wether Fell on to reach the walled track of Cam High Road (Roman Road).

3. Cross over Cam High Road and take the FP directly opposite (SP 'Marsett'). Follow the narrow path bearing to the left across the grassy moorland down to quickly join a clear grassy track across your path - turn left along this track and follow it on to reach a gate in a wall. After this gate, continue straight on along the grassy track heading across the wide, flat ridge of land with Raydale down to your right, on over a tumbledown wall just after which the track divides - follow the left-hand branch (SP) straight on to reach a crossroads of paths (SPs) near to the limestone outcrops of Green Scar, topped by a tumbledown wall. Continue straight on along the grassy path ahead (ignore footpaths down to the left and right) heading across the ridge of land, through two more gates after which follow the path bearing down to the right (Semerwater comes into view). This quickly becomes a sunken path that slants steeply down beneath the scars of Crag Hill, winding down through two gates on to reach Crag Side Road after a third gate. Turn right down along the road to reach a road-junction on the edge of Countersett - turn right at this junction then immediately left towards 'Stalling Busk' (1:4 hill) and follow this steeply down to reach Semerwater Bridge over the River Bain (Semerwater to your right).

4. Take the FP to the left immediately after Semerwater Bridge (SP 'Bainbridge') and follow the clear riverside path straight on, through a gate after which continue on along the riverside path over a stile then follow the river as it swings round to the right on to reach a ladder stile beside a gate in a wall. Head over the stile and follow the wide grassy path gradually climbing up the hillside to reach a wall-stile beside another gate, after which head straight on through two

more squeeze-stiles then head straight on up over the hill ahead (Bracken Hill), with the steep wooded gorge of the River Bain down to your left, to reach a wall-gate in the far top right-hand corner of the field. After the wall-gap, head straight on along the wide grassy path heading down then, as you approach the stone wall (and road) to your right, head down alongside this stone wall on your right (River Bain now down to your left again) to join the main road just above Bainbridge. Turn left along this road down into Bainbridge.

5. Leave Bainbridge along the road to the right of the Rose & Crown pub (road-sign 'Askrigg') and follow this road down to reach Yore Bridge across the River Ure. Immediately after the bridge take the FP to the left (SP), after which bear up to the right through a kissing gate (beside a gate in the fence) then head straight on over the old railway line to pass to the right of the farm buildings ahead (Yorescott Farm). Head through a small gate (beside a larger gate) just after the farmhouse then walk behind the farmhouse and on to quickly join the road through another small gate beside the main farm entrance. Turn left along the road then take the FP to the right after about 100 yards (SP 'Skell Gill'). Head straight on across the field to reach the wall opposite, however turn left here alongside the wall on your right (do not head through the gate in the wall). Where this wall bends round to the right (waymarker), head up to the left to a wall-gap (by a large tree), after which head to the right and walk along the top of the small hill alongside the overgrown hedge / tumbledown wall on your right to reach a wall-gap. After this wall-gap continue straight on across the field through another wall-gap, after which (where the wall bends away down to the right) bear to the right slanting down across the hillside, through a wall-gap in the wall across your path (in the wall which is heading down the hillside - farmhouse across to your right). After this, head on bearing slightly to the right, through two wall-stiles just to the left of the barn (and the farmhouse) that leads onto a walled lane.

6. Turn right along the lane, bending round to the left passing the farmhouse climbing up along the grassy / stony enclosed track to

reach a gate. After the gate continue along the grassy track as it bends round and up to the right (alongside the wall on your right) then, where the track levels out, turn left back on yourself slightly (three-finger SP 'Sedbusk') away from the wall across the grassy moorland and drop down to join a clearer grassy track alongside a wall on your left. Follow this clear grassy track straight on with the wall on your left through a series of gates passing three old farmhouses until you eventually join a clear stony track just before the large double gable-ended farmhouse of West Shaw Cote Farm.

7. Head straight on passing behind the farmhouse - *follow the permissive footpath (avoiding the farmyard) that runs parallel to the track behind the farmhouse* - the permissive path re-joins the grassy track just beyond the farmyard. Continue straight on along the grassy track again alongside the wall on your left. The track heads on through a series of gates and passes a small stone barn just after which it joins a clear enclosed walled track. Follow this walled track straight on then, after a short distance before this walled track bends round to the left, take the FP to the right over stone steps beside a gate. Turn left after these steps and walk straight on across the field, keeping close to the wall on your left, over a small stream to reach a small wall-gate, after which head straight on following the path through a series of wall-gates to reach the houses at Litherskew.

8. At Litherskew, you join a grassy / stony track which you follow straight on for a short distance then, where this track bends up to the right towards a house, follow the grassy track branching off to the left (SP) passing between the farm buildings to reach a gate just after the barn on your right (ignore gate and grassy track to the left). After the gate, head straight on through a wall-gate ahead and continue on across a series of fields through wall-gaps - as you approach the houses of Sedbusk (in the distance) follow the path bearing slightly to the left across the field that leads through a squeeze-stile into a copse of woodland. Walk through the woods then where you emerge from the woods continue straight on alongside the wall on your right to a wall-gate ahead that leads on to reach a lane at Sedbusk.

9. Turn left along the lane down out of Sedbusk then, after a short distance, take the FP to the right (where the stone wall enclosing the road opens out slightly) through a small wall-gate. Head diagonally down across the field, through a wall-gate then continue on dropping down to join the road through another small wall-gate. At the road take the path opposite to the right (SP 'Haylands Bridge') and follow the clear path bearing to the right down across the field, over a small stone bridge and on to reach the road. Turn left along the road, over Haylands Bridge and follow the road bearing round to the left heading up towards Hawes, however, take the flagged path to the right (SP 'Hawes, Pennine Way') through a kissing gate which quickly leads on to join the road again which you follow straight on up into the centre of Hawes.

Hardraw Force

Hawes Walking Weekend
- Sunday Walk -
Hawes, Sedbusk, Hardraw
& Appersett Viaduct

WALK INFORMATION

Highlights	A riverside ramble, the moorland village of Sedbusk, countless squeeze-stiles, a fine country house hotel, England's highest waterfall, following the Pennine Way and the magnificent Appersett Viaduct.
Distance	6 miles Time 3 hours
Maps	OS Explorer OL30
Refreshments	Pubs at Hawes, Simonstone and Hardraw. There are Tea Rooms at Hardraw.
Terrain	Field paths lead up to Sedbusk then on across a flat shelf of land through a succession of squeeze-stiles to reach Simonstone. Clear paths then drop down to Hardraw (famous waterfall) from where a stony track (Pennine Way) climbs Bluebell Hill before dropping down across pastures to reach Appersett. A quiet lane then leads up beneath Appersett Viaduct before clear field paths lead back to Hawes.
Ascents	Bluebell Hill - 315 metres above sea level
Caution	This walk involves a fairly steep climb up along a stony track onto Bluebell Hill. Take care when walking along the lanes around Appersett.

POINTS OF INTEREST

Upper Wensleydale is cradled by high fells with numerous attractive villages set high above the valley. It is quite a brisk walk up to the hill-village of Sedbusk, set beneath the gleaming limestone scars of Stags Fell. This attractive village is certainly 'off the beaten track' with only narrow lanes leading up to it. From its small green, a footpath strikes westwards across a flat shelf of land to reach Simonstone; if there is any footpath that symbolises the unique wall patterns of the Yorkshire Dales then this is it for in the space of a mile you have to negotiate at least fifteen wall-gap as you cross a succession of long and narrow fields. From Simonstone, with its elegant hotel, a path leads down to Hardraw where you will find Hardraw Force, England's highest waterfall. To see the waterfall you have to go into the pub (a good enough reason), as this privately owned waterfall is in the grounds of the Green Dragon Inn. It is well worth the effort as Hardraw Beck cascades for almost 100-ft in a single column of water into a plunge pool set in a huge natural amphitheatre of overhanging rocks and trees. It is possible to walk behind the waterfall, although this is very dangerous due to the large rocks precariously poised above your head. This large ravine provides the perfect acoustics for the annual Hardraw Scar Brass Band competition.

A stony track leads steadily up out of Hardraw bound for the summit of Great Shunner Fell, however, we turn off at Bluebell Hill down to reach Appersett leaving only hardy Pennine Way walkers to tackle the climb to the summit. The railway arrived in Upper Wensleydale during the 1870's. Hawes was the terminus of the NER Wensleydale line from Northallerton, which opened in 1878. From here the railway linked up with the Midland Railway Company's Settle and Carlisle Railway via a branch line from Garsdale Head. The railway closed completely in 1964, however, the section from Leeming to Redmire has recently been re-opened and there are efforts to re-instate the line all the way to Garsdale Head. Our route passes beneath the impressive Appersett Viaduct, its five arches rising high above the tumbling Widdale Beck.

For more information about the Wensleydale Railway, see Walking Weekend 2

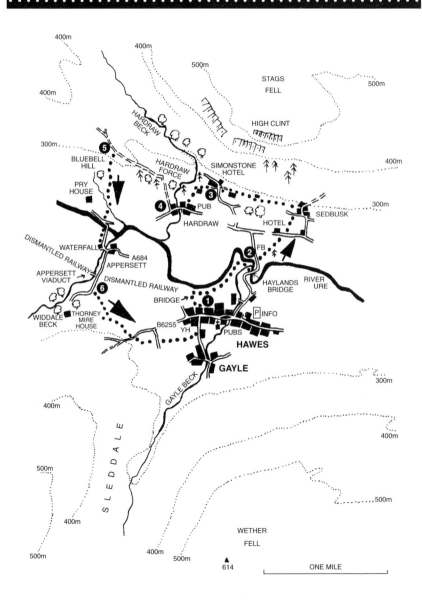

THE WALK

1. From the centre of Hawes, walk up through the Market Place along the main road through Hawes (passing the Crown Hotel and the Board Inn) then turn right along a lane to the side of 'Littlefairs' ironmongers and builders merchants. Follow the lane down then, at the houses, turn left to a small gate beside a garage. Head across the field through the wall-gate ahead, after which bear to the right down across two fields then pass through a tunnel through the embankment beneath the old railway line. Head straight on to reach the River Ure. Turn right and follow the riverside path on over two wooden stiles, then continue on following the river as it bends round to the left, over a series of metal ladder stiles (walking along the riverside levee) then follow the FP to the right (SP) across pastureland away from the river, over a FB across Gayle Beck then on to join the road beside Haylands Bridge.

2. Turn left over Haylands Bridge across the River Ure then follow the road round to the left alongside the river then, where the road leaves the river behind, take the FP to the right (SP 'Sedbusk'). Follow the clear path on across the field, over a stone bridge then up across fields to reach the road. At the road, take the FP opposite to the right (SP 'Sedbusk Lane') and head straight up the hillside - ignore the path to the right. Follow the clear path up over a wall-stile, then up passing to the left of a barn and onto a lane. Turn right along the lane into Sedbusk then where the road forks (by the VR postbox set into the wall), turn left up into the heart of the village. At the red telephone box, turn left across the small village green and head along the path passing in between the houses (SP 'Simonstone'). Follow the clear path straight on across several fields through a succession of wall-gaps, passing a bungalow (ignore the track) and continue on across more fields through more wall-gaps to join a clear farm track beside some large barns, which you follow straight on to join the road at Simonstone.

3. Turn left along the road then almost immediately right along the driveway towards Simonstone Hall Hotel. Where the lane bends up to the right towards the entrance to the hotel, take the FP to the left through a small wall-gate (just before the hotel's gardens) and follow this path straight on (with the wall / gardens to your right), through a squeeze-stile then on to reach West House Farm. Head through the small wall-gate (beside a larger red gate) just to the right of the farmhouse, then follow the clear path down to the left (flagged in places) to emerge at Hardraw beside the Green Dragon Inn *(England's highest waterfall accessible through the pub - small fee payable)*.

4. Turn right along the road passing the Green Dragon Inn on your right, over the bridge and head out of the village. Immediately after the last houses turn right along a stony track (SP 'Thwaite, Pennine Way, Cotterdale, Fossdale Moss'). Follow the walled track out of the village climbing steadily up, then round to the left after which the track levels out slightly passing a plantation on your left. Continue on along the track, climbing gradually up again, then where the track begins to bend round to the right up towards a gate across the track take the FP to the left through a gate (SP 'New Bridge').

5. After the gate, head immediately to the left following the narrow path down the hillside keeping close to the wall on the left down to reach a ladder stile in the bottom left-hand corner of the field. Cross over the stile then head straight on bearing very slightly to the left down along the grassy path, passing a SP, then continue straight on across the side of the hill to reach a wooden gate in a wall. After this gate, drop down the hillside to the gate ahead in the wall then head straight on across the field to reach the main A684 at a road junction. At the road, follow the main road to the left (SP 'Hawes, Leyburn') to quickly reach New Bridge ('Weak Bridge'), immediately after which follow the FP on the right that runs parallel with the main road up to reach Appersett. Walk over the bridge into Appersett, immediately after which take the lane to the right which runs up alongside Widdale Beck (11-ft height sign) and

follow this up to reach Appersett Viaduct. Pass beneath the viaduct and continue up along the road then, where the road bends to the right, take the FP to the left through a gate (SP 'Ashes').

6. Head straight on up across the rough field (waymarkers) then drop down to a wall-stile beside a gate (just to the right of a copse of woodland). Head up passing to the left of a roofless barn, a short distance after which turn right (SP 'Lanacar Lane') over a stile and up through a gap in a wall. After the wall-gap, turn left (alongside the wall on your left) to quickly join a clear grassy track - follow this track straight on then bending round to the right (following the wall on your left) on to join the B6255. At the road, turn left (take care) then almost immediately take the FP to the right (SP 'Gayle, Hawes'). Head up passing to the right of the ruined barn, immediately after which turn left through a squeeze-stile and follow the clear path across two fields to reach Mossy Lane. At the road take the FP opposite and follow the clear path across fields, through squeeze-stiles then passing a barn, after which continue straight on dropping down to join the road through a small wall-gate opposite the Wensleydale Creamery Visitor Centre. Cross over the road and take the FP opposite through a gate just to the left of the Creamery Visitor Centre that leads across a field then down across a car park, from where steps lead down from the far right-hand corner back into the centre of Hawes.

HORTON-IN-RIBBLESDALE

Ribblesdale

Horton lies on flat pastures along the valley floor at the heart of Ribblesdale on either side of the River Ribble, indeed, the name 'horton' means 'settlement on muddy ground'. There are three distinct parts to this straggling village. Firstly, the cluster of houses around St Oswald's Church, which dates from the early 1100's with some superb Norman stonework, although the tower is 14th Century. Then there is the junction of lanes, houses and the Crown Inn beside the twin stone bridges across the Ribble and Brants Ghyll. Nearby is the famous Pen-y-ghent Café, traditional 'clocking in and out' point for hardy walkers on the gruelling Three Peaks Walk, a 25-mile circuit taking in all three summits of Pen-y-ghent, Whernside and Ingleborough within twelve hours. Finally, there is Horton Station on the famous Settle and Carlisle Railway, one of the world's great railway journeys (for more information about this railway, please see Walking Weekend 4). The number one reason why people come to Horton-in-Ribblesdale is to walk. Pen-y-ghent rises dramatically above the village, beckoning you to climb its rugged shoulders onto its flat summit plateau, some 694 metres above sea level. It is actually comprised of a 'cap' of millstone grit on a layer of shales and sandstones which in turn lies on a huge shelf of Great Scar Limestone that dominates the scenery in this area. It is these layers of rocks that give the mountain its unmistakable profile, which is said to resemble a crouching lion. The name of this mountain is derived from the old Celtic words meaning the 'hill of the winds'; when you climb to the top, you will find out why! This is also 'limestone country' par excellence with crags, limestone pavements, dry valleys and potholes all around.

THE VILLAGE

Horton-in-Ribblesdale serves the needs of Three Peak walkers and boasts a large car park, toilets, shop, Post Office, campsites, Railway Station, café, outdoor shop, information point, B&B's and two pubs.

ACCOMMODATION

Tourist Information Centre, Settle: 01729 825192

HORTON PUBS

Crown Inn, Horton: **01729 860209**

The Pennine Way passes the front door of this popular walkers' pub, although only the foolish would do so. Inside, the cosy bar and traditional lounge boast a lovely open fire and oak beams that are said to have come from a sailing ship.

Golden Lion Hotel, Horton: **01729 860206**

Overlooking the historic Norman church, this large hotel is a popular haunt of walkers and cavers. Inside there are three rooms including a traditional tap room with a stone-flagged floor where muddy boots are welcome! The comfortable lounge boasts interesting bric-a-brac including a collection of blow torches.

PUBS ON THE WALKS

Helwith Bridge Hotel: 01729 860220

Horton Walking Weekend
- Saturday Walk -
Horton, Pen-y-ghent, Plover Hill, Foxup Road & Hull Pot

WALK INFORMATION

Highlights   Climbing the crouching lion, magnificent views, a long ridge walk, the haunt of the plover, an exciting descent to the upper reaches of Littondale, the old green lane of Foxup Road and an impressive pothole.

Distance	8.5 miles	Time	4 hours

Maps   OS Explorer OL2

Refreshments   Pubs, café and shop at Horton. No facilities on this walk - take provisions with you.

Terrain   Clear paths lead to the summit of Pen-y-ghent, however, the final climb is steep with some scrambling over rocks and steep drops to the side of the path. The flat summit plateau is exposed to the elements. The walk across the wide ridge to Plover Hill is boggy in places, whilst the descent down to join Foxup Road includes a short steep path down across rocky outcrops. The remainder of this walk follows clear tracks.

Ascents: Pen-y-ghent - 694 metres above sea level

Caution   This is a strenuous walk to the summit of Pen-y-ghent, with steep, rocky paths in places and boggy paths across high moorland. Do not attempt this walk in bad weather. Take a compass and OS map with you. Danger - keep away from the edge of Hull Pot. Limestone is slippery when wet.

POINTS OF INTEREST

Pen-y-ghent dominates Horton-in-Ribblesdale, rising dramatically above the rooftops. The long climb to its summit is superb, especially the final pull up its southern edge with short scrambles up rocky paths and vertigo-inducing views! From this vantage point 2,273-ft above sea level there is a breath-taking vista of mountains and dales with Littondale to the east and Pen-y-ghent's sister mountains of Ingleborough (724m) and Whernside (736m) to the west. The name of this mountain is derived from the old Celtic words meaning the 'hill of the winds' - very apt indeed! From its summit, a fine walk then ensues along a wide boggy ridge of moorland up onto Plover Hill. This broad mass of peat hags and bog pools rises to over 680 metres at the head of Littondale. The views are of distant hills including the Lakeland fells, Howgill Fells, Upper Wharfedale and Upper Littondale. A path leads gently down to reach an abrupt escarpment on its northern edge with wonderful views across Foxup Beck at the very head of Littondale, whilst the distinctive flat-top mountain of Ingleborough can be seen on the horizon to the west.

An old green lane known as Foxup Road is joined near the bottom of this valley, which is then followed all the way back to Horton. This old grassy track has been in constant used for centuries as a trading route between Littondale and Ribblesdale. At Swarth Gill Gate the track crosses the watershed between Ribblesdale and Littondale where a small section of boggy ground is all that separates rainwater from flowing eastwards into the North Sea or westwards into the Irish Sea. On Horton Moor, the track passes Hull Pot, an immense cavity in the earth some 60-ft feet deep by 300-ft wide. Hull Pot Beck flows into this chasm through a cave near the boulder strewn floor, however, after heavy rain the stream thunders over the lip of the pothole - this great hole in the ground has been known to fill up completely after very heavy rain!

HORTON SATURDAY WALK

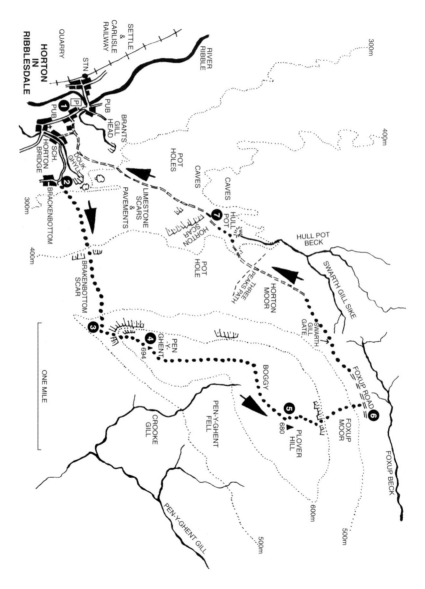

108

1. From the Car Park at Horton-in-Ribblesdale, turn right along the main road passing the Pen-y-Ghent Café and follow the road bending to the left around St Oswald's Church towards 'Settle' then, immediately after the churchyard on your left, take the turning to the left just before Horton Bridge across Horton Beck ('Dead End' sign). Follow this road up alongside the stream on your right then, as you approach the end of the lane, cross the FB to the right after which turn left up along the lane passing the school and on out of the village. Continue up along the lane with the wooded stream on your left at first then winding up to reach the hamlet of Brackenbottom.

2. As you approach Brackenbottom turn left through the gate before the farm buildings (SP 'Pen-y-ghent') and walk up to a stile beside a metal gate. Cross the stile then turn left and head up alongside the wall on your left. A clear path leads up across the hillside (with the wall on your left all the way), over a succession of wall stiles then up across the low limestone 'ridges' of Brackenbottom Scar (some scrambling required) and then up a clear stone path to reach a double ladder stile over a wall on the southern 'shoulder' of Pen-y-ghent with the rock outcrops of its summit up to your left.

3. Cross this stile and turn sharp left up towards the mountain. The clear stone-pitched path now climbs steeply up with a short scramble onto a small flat 'ridge' before another steep climb (pitched stone path) with more scrambling across rocks to reach the summit plateau. A clear path leads straight on rising gently up to reach the summit Trig Point and stone-built wind shelter.

4. Cross the wall-stile beside the wind shelter then turn immediately right alongside the wall on your right (SP 'Foxup Road') and follow this straight on across the summit ridge. After a short distance, the wall bends to the left down a short but steep 'step' before levelling out - continue straight on across the wide ridge (still with the wall

on your right) to reach a ladder stile over a wall across your path. Cross the ladder stile and continue straight on alongside the wall then follow the wall as it bends sharply round to the right and begins to rise up across boggy ground (peat hags) to reach a ladder stile in a wall corner (SP) on the rounded summit plateau of Plover Hill.

5. Cross the stile and turn immediately left (SP 'Foxup Road') alongside the short section of wall on your left at first (which very quickly turns away) then head straight on along the wide grassy path across the summit plateau for a short distance before the path drops down and bears slightly to the right to join the wall on your right at the top of a rocky escarpment. Follow the narrow path slanting steeply down to the left across this escarpment (take care - steep drops) then over a wall at the foot of the escarpment after which follow the grassy path gently dropping down keeping fairly close to the wall on your right to reach the rough grassy track of Foxup Road across your path at a gate in the wall on your right.

6. Turn left along this rough grassy track (SP 'Horton-in-Ribblesdale') and follow it on through a gate in a wall then continue on along the grassy track, with the flanks of Plover Hill rising steeply up to your left. The grassy track soon becomes a clearer wide stony path, which you follow straight on to reach a small stone FB across Swarth Gill Sike where the path joins a stone wall on your left (this is known as Swarth Gill Gate). Follow the clear stony path straight on alongside the wall on your left and through another gate across your path after about 0.5 miles after which the path becomes a rough grassy track again. Carry straight on along this grassy track alongside the wall on your left for a further 0.5 miles then, where the wall turns sharp left heading up the flanks of Pen-y-ghent, carry straight on along the wide grassy track over the eroded path of the Three Peaks Walk then straight on gently dropping down - the path soon becomes much clearer which you follow bearing to the right down alongside a small stream. This stream soon disappears down a pothole, however, continue on along the clear path to reach a ladder stile over a wall just before the large pothole of Hull Pot. Cross the

ladder stile then follow the grassy path to the left (keep away from the edge of Hull Pot) and follow this on to reach a gate at the top of the walled stony track of Horton Scar Lane (SP 'Horton').

7. Head through the gate and follow the walled stony track of Horton Scar Lane for just under 2 miles as it gradually drops down back towards Horton-in-Ribblesdale. As you approach the village, the track divides - follow the right-hand track down to reach the main road where you turn right back to the Car Park.

Horton Church

Horton Walking Weekend
- Sunday Walk -
Horton, Dub Cote, Long Lane,
Helwith Bridge & the River Ribble.

WALK INFORMATION

Highlights	Quiet tracks and old green lanes, wonderful views across Ribblesdale, the Settle and Carlisle Railway and rambling alongside the Ribble.
Distance	6 miles Time 3 hours
Maps	OS Explorer OL2
Refreshments	Pubs at Horton and Helwith Bridge. Café at Horton.
Terrain	Quiet country lanes lead to the isolated farm of Dub Cote from where grassy tracks lead up to join Long Lane (track). This track then heads gently down, grassy at first then stony, all the way to reach the main road at Helwith Bridge. A clear riverside path then leads back all the way to Horton.
Ascents:	Long Lane - 400 metres above sea level
Caution	The long and steady climb up to join Long Lane is exposed to the elements. Take care when crossing the B6479 at Helwith Bridge.

POINTS OF INTEREST

The old track of Long Lane, now a grassy track for most of the way, leads up across the southern shoulder of Pen-y-ghent bound for Silverdale. This is a wonderful old track with superb views across Ribblesdale. Across the valley, and in view for part of this walk, are three large and unsightly quarries. Horton Quarry is the largest, with sheer rock faces and deep workings. A valuable source of local employment, such large-scale industrial devastation is nevertheless hard to justify within the setting of a National Park especially as it is cutting into the pristine limestone pavements of Moughton. The quarried crushed limestone is used as aggregate in concrete, road building and in the construction industry. Ironically, the very landscape that people flock in their thousands to see is being ripped away to provide more roads to make it easier and quicker for people to get here. The quarries do not detract from this walk as there is plenty of interest to divert attention and, seen from close quarters as you near the end of this walk, the quarry rock face is quite dramatic.

From Helwith Bridge, where the bridge spans both the railway and the river, a delightful riverside path leads all the way back to Horton. Most of the main rivers in the Yorkshire Dales flow eastwards to drain into the Ouse, Humber and, ultimately, the North Sea. The Ribble is different. Streams gather in the wilderness of Newby Head Moss above Gearstones in the shadow of Whernside to form the infant Ribble which then flows south lapping the feet of Pen-y-ghent and passing through the old market town of Settle before turning west for the Irish Sea.

For more information about Settle and Carlilse Railway
please see Walking Weekend 4

HORTON SUNDAY WALK

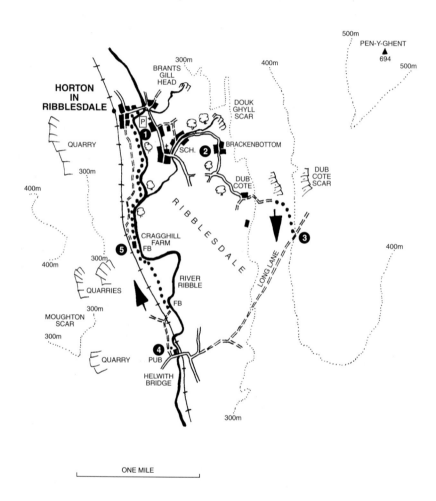

HORTON
IN
RIBBLESDALE

BRANTS GILL HEAD

DOUK GHYLL SCAR

BRACKENBOTTOM

QUARRY

SCH.

DUB COTE

DUB COTE SCAR

RIBBLESDALE

CRAGGHILL FARM
FB

RIVER RIBBLE

FB

QUARRIES

MOUGHTON SCAR

QUARRY

PUB

HELWITH BRIDGE

LONG LANE

PEN-Y-GHENT
694

500m
500m
300m
400m
400m
400m
400m
300m
300m
300m
300m
300m
300m

ONE MILE

THE WALK

1. From the Car Park at Horton-in-Ribblesdale, turn right along the main road passing the Pen-y-Ghent Café a short distance after which turn left (just before the Post Office) along a track (SP 'Foxup, Pen-y-ghent') and follow this walled stony track up out of the village to soon reach a gate across the track. Head through the gate, just after which the track forks - turn sharp right along a walled stony track and follow this down through a farmyard to reach a road, with Horton Beck just in front of you. Turn right then immediately left over a FB across the stream, after which follow the lane to the left passing the school and on out of the village. Continue up along the lane with the wooded stream on your left at first then winding up to reach the hamlet of Brackenbottom.

2. Continue along the lane through the hamlet then follow it on for a further 0.25 miles to reach a T-junction, where you turn left winding gradually up to reach the farmhouse of Dub Cote, where the metalled lane becomes a stony track. Turn left (SP 'Pen-y-ghent') along the stony track up through the farmyard (passing in front of the farmhouse) then straight on up along the stony track winding up to reach a ladder stile beside a gate. Head through this gate then follow the rough grassy track bearing to the right up across the field then bending to the left to re-join the wall on your left which you follow up to reach a gate / ladder stile in the top left-hand corner of the field. Head over this ladder stile and walk up alongside the wall on your left for a short distance then, just after the gate in the wall on your left, follow the clear grassy track bearing to the right slanting up across the hillside to reach a tumbledown wall towards the top right corner of the field (SP). Head through the gap in this wall to join the clear grassy track of Long Lane on the other side of the wall.

3. Turn right along this track and follow it down through two gates, after which the track becomes enclosed by stone walls - follow this very clear track gradually dropping down to reach a 'junction' with another stony track after 0.75 miles. Turn right (SP 'Helwith Bridge') and follow this clear stony track down to join the B6479, which you follow to the left then, after a short distance, take the turning to the right towards 'Austwick, Helwith Bridge'. Follow this road on over Helwith Bridge across the railway line and the River Ribble, immediately after which turn right along the footpath (SP 'Foredale') across the Helwith Bridge Hotel car park and over a stile beside a gate. Head straight on across two fields to join a metalled lane (caution - quarry traffic).

4. Turn right along this lane then, where it bends sharp left, head off to the right along a track through a gate that leads beneath a railway bridge. Follow this clear track straight on then bending to the right to reach the banks of the River Ribble. Follow this clear riverside path straight on (do not cross the FB) then, where the river bends to the right after a short distance, carry straight on along the clear enclosed overgrown path to reach a ladder stile beside a gate in the wall at the end of the enclosed path (open field ahead). Head straight on across the field bearing very slightly to the left (heading towards Cragghill Farm) to join a riverside track in the top left corner of the field, which you follow to the left (with the river on your right) to reach Cragghill Farm.

5. Head straight on through two gates across the edge of the farmyard (ignore the bridge to your right) then follow the very clear riverside path straight on heading along the wooded riverbank and across fields over a series of stiles (keep to the riverside path with the river on your right all the way) for 1.25 miles to reach the road (via some stone steps) near the bridge across the River Ribble at Horton-in-Ribblesdale. Turn right over the FB (or follow the road to the right over two bridges) back to the car park.

KETTLEWELL

Wharfedale

It was 'Ketel', a Norse-Irish chieftain who first settled in the sheltered valley at the confluence of Cam Gill Beck and the River Wharfe back in about the 9th Century, however, the village grew in size mainly due to its location. The Roman Road from Ilkley to Bainbridge came this way, as did the monastic route through to Coverham Abbey, the stagecoach route from London as well as numerous packhorse trails – it also lay on the edge of the Norman hunting forest of Langstrothdale Chase, and the monks of Coverham Abbey, Fountains Abbey and Bolton Priory held lands nearby. With so many important routes converging at one place Kettlewell quickly developed as a trading centre and gained its market charter in the 13th Century. Lead mining in the hills behind Kettlewell and textiles brought prosperity to the village with many of the houses being rebuilt or improved during the height of this industrial activity in the 18th and 19th centuries. Soon, a bustling village grew with as many as thirteen inns to accommodate the market-goers, miners and travellers. The old tracks, miner's paths and roads that radiate from the village in every direction make Kettlewell an excellent centre for walking and its three remaining inns are busy with a mixture of locals and walkers.

THE VILLAGE

Kettlewell is a thriving village with a garage, Youth Hostel, campsite, B&B's, tea rooms, craft shop, outdoor shop, Post Office, general stores, toilets, car park and three pubs.

ACCOMMODATION

National Park Information Centre, Grassington: 01756 751690

KETTLEWELL PUBS

Kings Head, Kettlewell: **01756 760242**
Tucked away in the heart of the village, the pub is always busy with a mixture of locals, visitors and walkers. It is a pub of great character with a stone-flagged floor, beams and a superb inglenook fireplace dominating the bar - the perfect place to dry out after a long walk as you can actually sit in the fireplace!

Blue Bell Hotel, Kettlewell: **01756 760230**
This attractive whitewashed inn dates back to 1680 and was once a coaching inn on the London to Richmond stagecoach route; the pub is named after an old stagecoach company. The interior retains a small traditional bar area warmed by an open fire, as well as several small dining areas. Watch the world go by from the benches at the front.

Racehorses Hotel, Kettlewell: **01756 760233**
This large hotel is situated directly opposite the Blue Bell and was once used as the stables - the name is reminiscent of the stagecoach days as the 'trace horses' were used to pull the coaches up the steep Park Rash Pass behind the village. The comfortable interior is divided into several rooms with some lovely old stone fireplaces.

PUBS ALONG THE WALKS

Fox & Hounds, Starbotton: 01756 760269
Falcon Inn, Arncliffe: 01756 770205

Kettlewell Walking Weekend
- Saturday Walk -
Kettlewell, Hag Dike, Great Whernside,
Great Hunters Sleets & Top Mere Road.

WALK INFORMATION

• •

Highlights	Ketel's village, England's highest chapel, the source of the Nidd, wonderful views, a Brigantes defensive ditch, monastic roads and one of the finest views in the Dales.
Distance	8.5 miles Time 4 hours
Maps	OS Explorer OL30
Refreshments	Pubs, cafés and shops at Kettlewell. No facilities en route - take plenty of provisions with you.
Terrain	Clear grassy paths lead steadily up from Kettlewell above Dowber Gill (steep drops to side of path) to reach Hag Dike Farm, from where a boggy path climbs steeply up across open moorland onto the summit ridge, with a scramble over boulders to get to the summit of Great Whernside (exposed to the elements). A boggy path follows the summit ridge before dropping steeply down along a rough path to reach the unfenced Coverdale road. Clear grassy moorland paths and tracks skirt around the head of Cam Gill Beck before a final steep descent along a stony track back into Kettlewell.
Ascents:	Great Whernside - 704 metres above sea level
Caution	This is a strenuous walk up to the summit of Great Whernside, with some steep sections across rough / rocky ground. Do not attempt this walk in bad weather. Take a compass and OS map with you.

POINTS OF INTEREST

Great Whernside dominates Upper Wharfedale, an immense mountainous shoulder of land towering above Kettlewell that forms a very physical boundary between Wharfedale and Nidderdale, indeed the River Nidd is born on its eastern flanks. From the flat, rocky plateau 704 metres above sea level there are incredible views across Wharfedale towards Kilnsey Crag, down along the length of Coverdale towards Leyburn and across the reservoirs of Upper Nidderdale. In every direction fells, hills and mountains rise up from deep valleys with Buckden Pike (702 metres) and Pen-y-ghent (694 metres) clearly visible. Great Whernside is capped by a huge shelf of gritstone, which sits on the underlying limestone strata - it is this gritstone that gave the mountain its name for Whernside means 'the hillside where millstones were got'. Great Whernside is often mistaken for Whernside above Ribblehead, which forms one of the famous Three Peaks of Yorkshire - why not make up your own mind as to which Whernside really is 'great' and spend a weekend at the Sportsman's Inn at Cowgill and walk up Ribbledale's Whernside to compare it (Walking Weekend 4)!

On the climb up to the summit of Great Whernside you come rather unexpectedly across the 18th Century farmhouse of Hag Dike, used as a Scout Hostel since 1947. This is one of the highest buildings in the country and even has a small chapel in a converted outbuilding that is said to be the highest chapel in England. A deep earthwork stretches for almost a mile across the saddle of land known as Great Hunters Sleets between Great Whernside and Buckden Pike. This is Tor Dike, a huge ditch and rampart that once formed part of a defensive system built by the early British Iron Age tribes, collectively known in the North of England as the Brigantes, in an attempt to prevent the Romans invading the northern Dales. The final part of this walk follows the old monastic route known as Top Mere Road between Coverham Abbey in Coverdale and Kettlewell, where the monks held grazing lands. This ancient walled lane forms a superb end to this walk with far-reaching views down Wharfedale towards Kilnsey and Grass Wood.

KETTLEWELL SATURDAY WALK

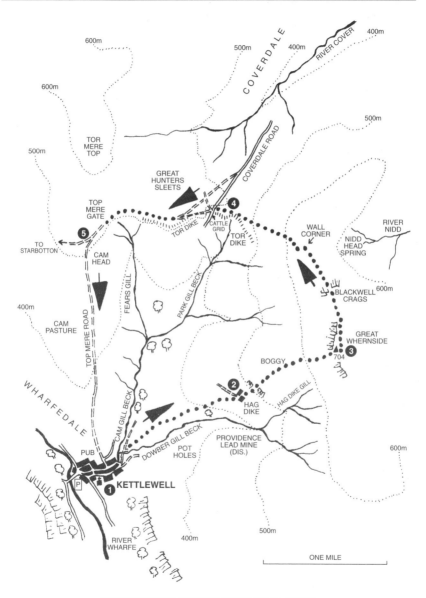

121

THE WALK

1. From the car park behind the garage near the bridge across the River Wharfe, turn left along the main road into the centre of Kettlewell bearing left over the bridge across Cam Gill Beck then turn right at the Blue Bell Inn and follow the lane up through the village to reach a junction with the General Stores on the corner. Turn right here, over another bridge then immediately left along a lane (Kings Head on your right). Follow this lane alongside Cam Gill Beck up to reach a small stone bridge to your left on the edge of the village. Do not cross this bridge, but continue straight on along the rough track (SP 'Hag Dyke, Providence Pot'), still with the stream on your left, to reach another stone bridge across Dowber Gill Beck. Cross this bridge then turn immediately right (SP 'Hag Dike') along a streamside path to quickly reach a wall-stile and gate to your left. Cross the stile then head straight on (SP 'Hag Dyke') along a wide grassy path climbing up alongside the wall on your left to reach a wall-stile at the top of the field. After this stile, carry straight on along the grassy path up through a gate in a wall, after which follow the path climbing quite steeply up to reach a ladder stile beside large wall-gap. Cross the stile then head straight on along the wide path up to reach an 'edge' of land high above Dowber Gill Beck (SP). The path now levels out and leads on through two bridlegates and over a ladder stile before climbing up again (SP) then bending to the right through a large gap in a wall up to reach Hag Dike.

2. Turn right through the gate into the yard of Hag Dike (SP 'Coverdale Road via Great Whernside') then follow the path immediately to the right of the old farm buildings through a small gate, then head left through another gate passing behind the old farmhouse along a distinct path climbing quickly but steeply up a rocky escarpment onto a flat plateau (surmounted by a line of stone cairns). Head straight on along the clearly waymarked path (marker posts) as it meanders across the gently rising boggy moorland - *boulder-strewn summit of Great Whernside directly ahead.* As you

approach the summit there is a final steep climb up across a rocky escarpment onto the summit plateau of Great Whernside with its large cairn and trig point.

3. At the trig point on the summit turn left and walk along the clear path across the flat plateau of Great Whernside keeping close to the rocky escarpment on your left. The path soon divides with a waymarked path slanting off to the left - our route continues straight on along the top of the rocky escarpment passing a large stone cairn, then a stone shelter and on to reach the conspicuous outcrop of Blackfell Crags. Continue straight on dropping gradually down across the wide 'shoulder' of land to reach the corner of a wall ahead. Cross the stile to the left in the corner of this wall and head down the hillside with the wall on your left, dropping gently at first then more steeply to quickly reach a stile on your left and a well-worn path. Follow this clear path to the right slanting steeply down the hillside then, where the grassy path levels out slightly at the bottom of this steep section, follow the clear path down to the left then straight on across boggy flat ground to reach a stile beside a gate in a wall across your path (Tor Dike on your left). After the wall stile, follow the path straight on to reach the unenclosed Coverdale road just to the right of a cattle grid.

4. Turn right along the unfenced road for just over 0.25 miles then, just after the tumbledown walls which once enclosed the road end, take the grassy track to the left back on yourself (SP 'Starbotton, Kettlewell'). Follow this clear grassy track gradually bearing away from the road heading across the open moorland of Great Hunters Sleets. After a while, the grassy track curves to the right (another track joins it from the left) then runs alongside a wall (Tor Dike on the other side of the wall) to reach a gate / stile in a wall corner. Head through the gate and continue on along the clear, undulating rough path alongside the wall on your left skirting around the valley head, through another gate (Top Mere Gate) and carry straight on to reach a fork in the track (junction of Starbotton Road with Top Mere Road).

5. At this junction, bear left (SP 'Kettlewell') and follow the clear track gently dropping down across the open moorland of Cam Head to reach a gate across your path after 0.5 miles. Continue straight on along the grassy track heading down across the moorland for a further 0.5 miles to reach another gate at the top of a walled stony track (Top Mere Road). Carry straight on along this walled track gradually dropping down (Wharfedale in the distance) before a final steep descent to join the metalled road on a sharp bend just above Kettlewell. Follow this road straight on steeply down into Kettlewell.

Kettlewell

Top:
Aysgarth Falls

Middle:
Bolton Castle

Bottom:
Linton - in - Craven

©Mark Reid

Top:
Norber Erratics

Middle:
Muker, Swaledale

Bottom:
Malham Cove

©Mark Reid

Top: Ribblehead Viaduct
Middle: Overlooking Kettlewell
Bottom: Roman Road, Wensleydale
©Mark Reid

Top: Haymeadow, Swaledale
Middle: Top Mere Road, Wharfedale
Bottom: Stake Road, Bishopdale
©Mark Reid

Kettlewell Walking Weekend
- Sunday Walk -
Kettlewell, Starbotton, Old Cote Moor, Arncliffe & Littondale

WALK INFORMATION

Highlights	A perfect glaciated valley, the stony bottom, ancient woodland, breathtaking views, windswept moorland, one of England's classic country pubs.
Distance	7.5 miles (*short route* 4.5 miles)
Time	3 hours
Maps	OS Explorer OL30
Refreshments	Pubs at Kettlewell, Starbotton and Arncliffe. Cafés and shops at Kettlewell.
Terrain	From Kettlewell to Starbotton, this walk follows clear field paths. The climb over Old Cote Moor to Arncliffe follows narrow paths up through woodland then rough tracks across moorland. The climb back over to Kettlewell is rough underfoot and steep in places.
Ascents:	Old Cote Moor - 520 metres above sea level Middlesmoor Pasture - 490 metres above sea level (*Short route:* Moor End Fell - 390 metres)
Caution:	This walk involves two long and steep climbs along rough tracks and paths crossing exposed moorland. The path up out of Starbotton includes a narrow section along the edge of an escarpment with steep drops to the side. The descent down into Kettlewell follows a steep rocky path down through a cleft in the crags - limestone is slippery when wet.

POINTS OF INTEREST

The walk between Kettlewell and Starbotton probably follows the line of the Roman road between their forts at Ilkley and Bainbridge, and provides the perfect opportunity to 'get your legs going' before the long climb over to Littondale! Starbotton's rather unusual name is derived from Anglo-Saxon words meaning 'stony valley bottom'. The flat valley floor in this part of Wharfedale is prone to flooding as the meandering river is fed by many fast-flowing streams that soon swell the waters after heavy rain.

The climb from Starbotton over Moor End Fell and Old Cote Moor is one of the finest 'inter-valley' walks in the Yorkshire Dales, with breathtaking views of the glaciated valley of the Wharfe. Coupled with this are remnants of ancient woodland, expansive moorland and gleaming limestone outcrops that combine to create a landscape of contrast and interest.

Arncliffe is an absolute delight with its large village green, ancient church and unchanged village pub, the perfect place to spend an hour before the climb back over to Kettlewell. Look out for the memorial to the local men who fought at the Battle of Flodden Field in 1513 inside Arncliffe Church. The highlight of this walk are the limestone crags of Gate Close Scar high above Kettlewell, which offer a bird's eye view of Kettlewell sheltering below the high fells of Great Whernside. The final descent is exciting as it drops down through a cleft in these crags and then follows a very steep and rocky path down - care must be taken on this section!

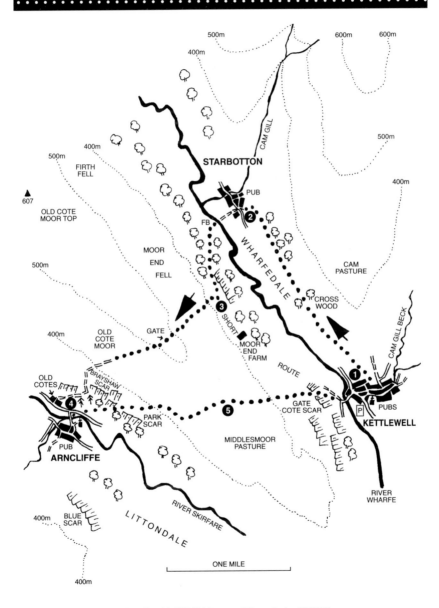

1. From the car park behind the garage near the bridge across the River Wharfe, turn left along the main road into the centre of Kettlewell bearing left over the bridge across Cam Gill Beck towards 'Buckden' then take the lane to the right immediately after the Blue Bell Inn. Follow this lane up then, where it bends sharply round to the right, head straight on along the stony track to the side of Cam Cottage (SP 'Starbotton'), which quickly becomes a clear path enclosed by walls that leads up to reach a stile across your path. After the stile, follow the wall curving up and round to the left along a clear grassy path which soon levels out - follow this clear path straight on heading across the steep hillside over a series of wall stiles, through woodland and across pastures for just over 1.5 miles. As you approach Starbotton (with the houses just down to your left), head left through a small wall-gate (SP) and head down across the field, through a gate to the right halfway down this field then follow the rough track down through another gate and onto a lane on the outskirts of Starbotton.

2. Turn left along the lane to quickly reach the main road where you take the walled path opposite to the right (SP 'Arncliffe, Kettlewell, Buckden'). Follow this path down to reach a large FB across the River Wharfe. After the FB, head straight on through the gate (SP 'Arncliffe') and follow the narrow path enclosed by stone walls / large trees ahead. The path bends round to the left just after a stone barn and climbs gently up to reach a gate across your path, after which continue straight on along the clear stony path slanting steeply up through woodland to eventually reach a bridle-gate at the top of the woods. The path now levels out slightly, with wonderful views across Wharfedale, rising gently up to a wall-gate at the top of the escarpment on Moor End Fell.

Short route: Head through the wall-gate then turn left (SP 'Kettlewell') through another gate in a wall just ahead, after which continue straight on across the field (heading towards Moor End Farm ahead), through another gate then, as you approach the end of the next field, head up to the right (SP) to a gate in the corner of the field. After this gate, turn left through another gate (SP) and head on skirting around the farmhouse and through the farmyard of Moor End Farm. Pass in front of the farmhouse and follow the track straight on leaving the farmhouse behind - follow this track straight on then, where Kettlewell comes into view, follow the clear track winding steeply down all the way to join the road just beside the road bridge across the River Wharfe on the outskirts of Kettlewell.

3. After the wall-gate follow the grassy path bearing up to the right (SP 'Arncliffe') skirting around a stone enclosure then climbing straight up the hillside of Moor End Fell up over a tumbledown wall then up over a low limestone ridge, after which the hillside levels out slightly - continue straight on gently climbing up to reach the left-hand corner of a stone wall at the top of the next low ridge. Carry on up the hillside with the wall on your right for a short distance and head through a wall gap then continue to follow the wall (now on your left) to reach a gate in a wall at the top of Old Cote Moor. After the gate, follow the clear stony path ahead bearing very slightly to the right gradually dropping down across the heather moorland. The track soon becomes a grassy track across limestone pastures that leads steadily down then winds more steeply down to reach a gate in a wall at the top of a steep bank above Arncliffe. Follow the stony track winding steeply down then head through the farmyard of Old Cotes to reach the road. Turn left along the road and follow it round to the right to reach the bridge across the River Skirfare *(Arncliffe short detour ahead)*.

4. As you reach the bridge across the Skirfare, take the riverside path to the left immediately before the bridge (SP 'Kettlewell') and follow this on to quickly join a road. At the road take the path opposite (SP 'Kettlewell') and follow this slanting steeply up the hillside to the right, over a wall stile then up through woodland scrambling up across limestone outcrops to reach a ladder stile at the

top of the wooded Park Scar. After the stile, follow the clear path to the right slanting up across the hillside over a ladder stile then continue on slanting up the hillside (limestone changes to gritstone), over a tumbledown wall then carry straight on along the clear path gently rising up across the hillside (Littondale steeply down to your right) then follow the path as it swings up to the left (SP) for the final climb up to a ladder stile after which it is a short walk to another ladder stile over a wall at the top of the wide ridge of moorland (Middlesmoor Pasture).

5. After this stile, head straight on bearing slightly to the right dropping down along a grassy path (Kettlewell comes into view just after a small limestone ridge) and follow the clear path dropping down (heading towards Kettlewell) bearing slightly to the right across the gently sloping grassy hillside to join a wall on your right (ignore the gate in this wall) which you follow down to soon reach a ladder stile across this wall. After the ladder stile, follow the clear grassy path to the left dropping down across the hillside (heading towards Kettlewell) to reach the top of the limestone escarpment of Gate Close Scar. A narrow path leads down through a cleft in this scar (take care) before dropping steeply down to reach a track which you follow to the right to join the road just above the bridge across the River Wharfe, which you follow into Kettlewell.

LANGTHWAITE

Arkengarthdale

*There is something very special about Arkengarthdale,
Yorkshire's most northerly dale. Its fells, hills and valleys are starkly
beautiful, wild and brooding. Old lead mines lie scattered across the hills,
scarring the landscape with spoil heaps, hushes, levels and tracks. You will
not find crowds of visitors here, only the occasional walker who comes to
appreciate this wondrous landscape. Langthwaite lies at the heart of this
valley, a cluster of old miners' cottages set around a small square with the
traditional Red Lion Inn tucked away near the narrow stone bridge that
will be familiar to many from the opening sequences of the TV series 'All
Creatures Great and Small'. The peculiarly northern name of this valley
originates from the time of the Vikings when Arkil, son of Gospatrick, owned
this land; a 'garth' is an enclosure and 'dale' a valley in Old Norse.
A handful of hamlets lies along the narrow valley floor, many of which
also have Old Norse names such as Storthwaite, Eskeleth, Whaw and
Faggergill; indeed, Langthwaite means the 'long clearing'. Arkengarthdale
was once one of the most productive lead mining areas in Britain,
especially during the 18th and 19th centuries. At their height the CB Mines
employed around 300 men, however, by the late 1800's most of the mines
had closed due to cheaper imports and dwindling reserves.*

THE VILLAGE

Langthwaite is a delightful village of stone-built cottages clustered around a small square beside Arkle Beck. It boasts two pubs, B&B's, a bus service, toilets, public telephone, small car park and an Information Board. The Red Lion Inn sells a wide selection of books as well as a limited amount of provisions.

ACCOMMODATION

National Park Information Centre, Reeth: 01748 884059.

LANGTHWAITE PUBS

The CB Inn, Langthwaite: **01748 884567**
The CB Inn is named after Charles Bathurst, Lord of the Manor during the 18th Century and the person responsible for developing many of the lead mines in the dale. The estate was sold to Dr John Bathurst in the mid 17th Century and remained in the Bathurst family for generations until the family link died out in 1912; Dr Bathurst was the physician to Oliver Cromwell. The pub is renowned for its good food, comfortable rooms and convivial bar.

The Red Lion Inn, Langthwaite: **01748 884218**
Traditional Dales' village pub, with cosy corners and well-kept beer. This pub has been featured in numerous films and TV programmes including All Creatures Great and Small. No Accommodation.

PUBS ALONG THE WALKS

Buck Hotel, Reeth: 01748 884210
Kings Arms, Reeth: 01748 884259
Black Bull Hotel, Reeth: 01748 884213

Langthwaite Walking Weekend
- Saturday Walk -
Langthwaite, Fremington Edge, Reeth & Arkle Beck

WALK INFORMATION

Highlights	Booze but no pub, the legacy of the lead mines, a bird's eye view of Arkengarthdale, following Fremington Edge, Yorkshire's White House, the 'capital' of Swaledale and following Arkle Beck upstream.
Distance	8.5 miles Time 4 hours
Maps	OS Explorer OL30
Refreshments	The Red Lion or CB Inn at Langthwaite or choice of three pubs, several shops and cafés at Reeth.
Terrain	Clear paths and tracks all the way, although good boots are required as many paths are stony and uneven. This walk involves a steep climb up onto Fremington Edge and then a steep descent down into Reeth. The path along the top of Fremington Edge is muddy underfoot and exposed to the elements. The 'return leg' follows field paths up along the valley floor.
Ascents	Booze - 340 metres above sea level Fremington Edge - 473 metres above sea level
Caution	The ascent and descent to and from Fremington Edge is steep in places. Do not explore the old lead mine workings.

POINTS OF INTEREST

Fremington Edge dominates the confluence of Arkengarthdale and Swaledale, a towering wall of shimmering scree slopes and crags that rise sheer from the flat valley floor - our objective for today's walk. Our route starts from Langthwaite, from where we climb up to the windswept hamlet of Booze with its derelict farmhouses set high on the hillside - the name 'booze' comes from the Old English word 'bowehouse' meaning 'house by the curve'. A delightful path drops down to the old farmhouse of Storthwaite Hall ('storthwaite' comes from Old Norse and means 'clearing of the bullocks') set at the foot of Slei Gill, which is badly scarred with the remains of lead mines. From Storthwaite Hall a path snakes its way steeply up onto the top of Fremington Edge through an area of old spoil heaps and workings of the disused Fell End Lead Mines. A large stone-built cairn stands at the edge of the escarpment from where there are breath-taking views across Arkengarthdale. A footpath leads across the top of Fremington Edge, with the vast expanse of heather-clad Marrick Moor stretching away to the east - the path runs alongside a stone wall that acts as a very convenient wind-break!

After just over a mile, we come to the old road over to Hurst, now just a rough stony track, which we follow steeply down to reach the whitewashed farmhouse of The White House - a well-known landmark - from where there is a superb bird's eye view of Reeth set on the gently sloping flanks of Calver Hill with Swaledale snaking away into the distance. From Reeth, field paths lead up through Arkengarthdale, keeping fairly close to Arkle Beck for most of the way, passing the 'twin' farms of East and West Raw Croft. This is easy walking, although the numerous squeeze-stiles provide a challenge! Dominating the scene are the dramatic limestone crags and screes of Fremington Edge, scarred with former lead mine spoil heaps.

LANGTHWAITE SATURDAY WALK

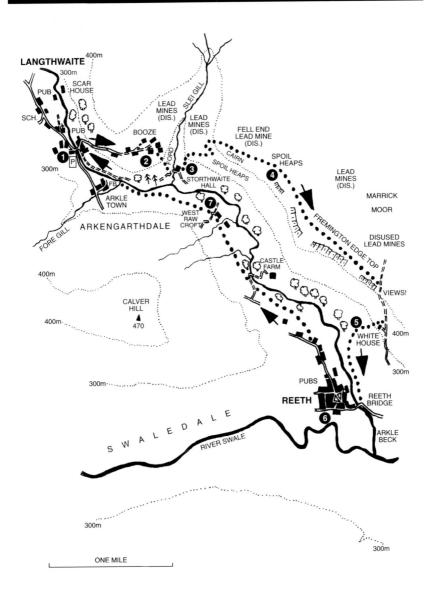

LANGTHWAITE

400m
300m

SCAR HOUSE

PUB

SCH.

PUB

BOOZE

LEAD MINES (DIS.)

SLEI GILL

LEAD MINES (DIS.)

FELL END LEAD MINE (DIS.)

CAIRN

SPOIL HEAPS

SPOIL HEAPS

LEAD MINES (DIS.)

MARRICK

MOOR

300m

STORTHWAITE HALL

ARKLE TOWN

WEST RAW CROFT

ARKENGARTHDALE

FORE GILL

FREMINGTON EDGE TOP

DISUSED LEAD MINES

VIEWS!

400m

CASTLE FARM

CALVER HILL

400m

470

WHITE HOUSE

400m

300m

300m

PUBS

REETH

REETH BRIDGE

ARKLE BECK

SWALEDALE

RIVER SWALE

300m

300m

ONE MILE

© Crown Copyright 2005. All rights reserved. Licence Number 100011978

139

THE WALK

1. From the car park at Langthwaite, turn right along the road then take the first turning to the right over the bridge into the centre of the village ('Red Lion Inn' sign). Head straight on along the lane and follow this climbing steeply up out of the village, winding up and bending round to the right. The road soon levels out with superb views across Arkengarthdale - continue along this road until you reach the scattered hamlet of Booze. Where the lane divides as you enter the hamlet, take the right-hand branch straight on and follow this down to reach Town Farm at the end of the track.

2. Head through the green metal gate into the farmyard then turn immediately right down through two more gates (to the side of the barn) out onto a field (SP). Head down across the field bearing slightly to the right, through a gate then continue on down across the field, through a small wall-gap then down to join a grassy track (SP) which you follow to the right to join a clear rough track at a gate. Turn left down along this track (SP 'Fremington) to quickly reach a ford / FB across Slei Gill, after which continue straight on along the track passing in front of the farm buildings of Storthwaite Hall then turn left through a gate immediately after the house (SP 'Hurst').

3. Follow the clear grassy track climbing up the hillside, initially enclosed by stone walls then climbing up across the open hillside (keeping close to the wall on your left) to reach a gate in a stone wall across your path. After the gate follow the clear stony track to the right (SP 'Hurst') climbing up through an area of old spoil heaps and workings (marker-posts) then bending up round to the left as you reach a line of crags and a large spoil heap. Follow the stony path climbing up then bending round to the right onto the shoulder of land of Fell End (the stony track becomes a grassy path). The grassy path now climbs gradually up (marked by small cairns) through an area of old spoil heaps (Fell End Lead Mine), passing a conspicuous

large cairn just across to your right on the very edge of the escarpment, to eventually reach a gate in a stone wall across your path.

4. Head through the gate and follow the path straight on alongside the stone wall on your right across the top of Fremington Edge for just over a mile to reach a rough track across your path (immediately before a gate in a wall across your path). Turn right along the track through a gate and follow this rough stony track dropping steeply down (Reeth comes into view), through a gate across the track then continue on dropping down then, just above the whitewashed farmhouse of The White House, turn right off the track along a grassy path (SP) passing above the farmhouse to reach a small gate in a stone wall. After the wall-gate, follow the winding grassy path steeply downhill to reach a small wall-gate next to a metal gate at the bottom of the field.

5. Head through the gate and carry straight on across the field passing a barn to reach a wall gap, then straight on again through another wall gap after which turn left and walk across the field (keeping close to the wall on your left) straight on to reach a wall-gap at the end of the field (do not go through the gate just before this to the left). After the wall-gap, head straight on across the next field passing to the left of a barn and through the left-hand of two gates (clearly marked) and follow the wall on your right to reach the road near to the garage at Reeth. Turn right along the road over Reeth Bridge and up into Reeth.

6. Leave Reeth along the road to the right-side of the Buck Hotel (SP 'Langthwaite, Barnard Castle, Arkengarthdale') and follow this up out of the village. After the cattle grid, follow the road bending round to the left (wide undulating grassy verge) then take the footpath to the right just beside the white gate of Sleights Brow House (SP). Head diagonally to the left across the field over a wall-stile, passing to the right of a brick-built barn, then straight on along the clear path across fields (Arkle Beck across to your right)

over a series of wall-stiles. You soon pass to the right of a larger stone-built barn then on over a small stream after which continue straight on along the clear path to join a clear farm track. Follow the track straight on through a gate then, where the track drops down towards the river, branch off to the left (SP 'Langthwaite') along a path to reach a squeeze-stile. Follow the clear path heading straight on up through the valley, with Arkle Beck down to your right, over a small stream then on to reach a gate. After this gate, head straight on alongside the stone wall on your right then, where this wall turns away to the right (East Raw Croft Farm down to your right), head through a squeeze-stile ahead then bear slightly to the right down through a small gate to pass above West Raw Croft Farm to join a track just beyond the farmhouse.

7. Head straight on along this farm track for a short distance then, where it bends sharply up to the left, head straight on to the right (on this sharp bend) along a grassy track keeping close to the wall on your right to quickly reach a gate in the bottom corner of the field. Head through the gate then straight on across the field along the grassy track keeping close to the wall on your right through a large gap in the wall (no gate) and continue on to reach another gate after which head diagonally left up the hill towards the telegraph pole and a signpost (approx. 75 yards below the telegraph pole). At the signpost, follow the clear path to the right crossing a tumbledown wall then straight on to reach a wall stile in the bottom right hand corner of the field. Continue straight on along the clear path over a number of stiles gradually bearing down across the undulating hillside (Arkle Beck down to your right) to join the wooded banks of Arkle Beck. Follow the clear riverside path straight on to reach a FB. Cross the FB then turn left along the clear riverside track which you follow back into Langthwaite to emerge out into the small square opposite the Red Lion Inn.

Langthwaite Walking Weekend
- Sunday Walk -
Langthwaite, Windegg Lead Mines, Seal Houses Moor & Whaw

WALK INFORMATION

Highlights	Wild heather moorland, wonderful views across the valley, limestone scars, abandoned lead mines, the old mines' villages of Whaw and Eskeleth, wooded riverbanks and a church built after battle.
Distance	7.5 miles
Time	3.5 hours
Maps	OS Explorer OL30
Refreshments	The Red Lion or the CB Inn at Langthwaite; no facilities en route.
Terrain	A mixture of quiet country lanes, moorland tracks and riverside paths. This walk crosses the open moorland of Peat Moor Green and Seal Houses Moor, with boggy paths and rough terrain.
Ascents:	Peat Moor Green - 460 metres above sea level
Caution:	This walk crosses the open moorland of Peat Moor Green and Seal Houses Moor, with boggy paths and rough terrain; navigation may be difficult in poor weather. Do not explore the old mine workings.

From Langthwaite, our route climbs up to the remote hamlet of Booze with its derelict farmhouses set high on the hillside from where an old track leads up across Scotty Hill and then skirts across the flanks of Peat Moor Hill passing beneath an impressive line of crags amidst old spoil heaps, with wonderful views across the upper reaches of Arkengarthdale. An old miners' path then turns off along Dry Gill Edge to reach the former Windegg Lead Mine with its poisoned spoil heaps, overgrown levels and deep hushes. From here, we head across the lower flanks of Seal Houses Moor high above Shaw Beck before dropping down to the hamlet of Whaw. A delightful riverside path now leads all the way back to Langthwaite with woodland, crags and meadows providing interest. The final stretch passes below the imposing shooting lodge of Scar House before reaching St Mary's Church, a rare example of a 'Waterloo Church' built using funds raised as thanksgiving for Napoleon's defeat.

Langthwaite Village featuring former village shop.

LANGTHWAITE SUNDAY WALK

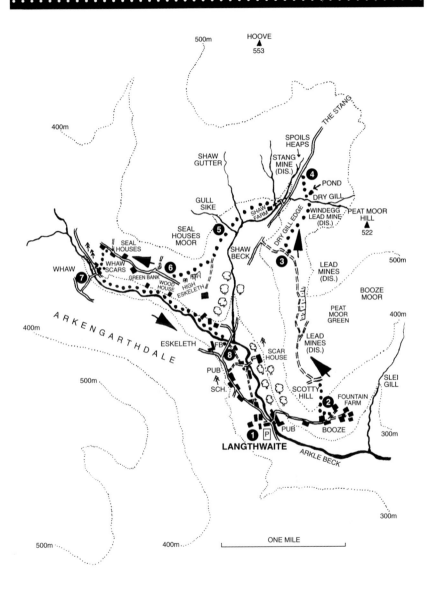

145

THE WALK

1. From the car park at Langthwaite, turn right along the road then take the first turning to the right over the bridge into the centre of the village ('Red Lion Inn'). Head straight on through the square then along the lane and follow this climbing steeply up out of the village, winding up and bending round to the right. After this initial climb, the road gradually rises up then levels out and passes a farmhouse on your right after which the road becomes a track which you follow straight on into the scattered hamlet of Booze. Where the lane divides as you enter the hamlet just by a derelict farmhouse, take the left-hand branch (towards 'Fountain Farm') and follow this lane up then after the next derelict farm on your left (immediately before the gate across the lane) turn left along a path passing behind the ruinous farmhouse (stone sign 'Scotty Hill, Booze Moor').

2. Follow this enclosed path up to quickly reach a bridle-gate, after which continue straight on then, where the walls open out, follow the track curving round to the right up to a gate in a wall. After the gate, head straight on along a sunken grassy path keeping close to the wall on your right and follow this up, running parallel to a track on your left for a while then, as you approach the top of the field, follow the wall bending to the right to quickly reach a stile beside a gate just above a barn in the adjacent field (ignore the track that leads up to a gate at the top of the field). After this stile, turn left to quickly join a clear moorland track which you follow to the left then, where it divides after a short distance (where the wall bends away to the left), follow the right-hand track heading straight on up across the moorland. Follow this track gradually rising up across the moor, then curving gently round to join a wall just across to your left. Continue straight on then, where the track divides, follow the left-hand track down to join the wall on your left. Follow this track alongside the wall then, after a short distance, the track bears away from the wall passing beneath crags and old workings up to your right after which continue along the track leaving these crags behind for a further 0.25 miles then, about 100 yards before the track bends

sharply down to the left, turn right off the track along an indistinct grassy track (following the curve of the steep hillside to your right).

3. Follow this track across the 'shelf' of land (Dry Gill Edge) along the foot of the steep hillside to your right to soon reach some overgrown workings with crags and screes up to your right. The grassy track now becomes an indistinct path - head straight on passing below these crags and scree slopes then bear very slightly to the left straight on across the rough open hillside to reach the overgrown spoil heaps and workings of Windegg Lead Mines. Pass to the left of the large spoil heap just after which cross the stream of Dry Gill then bear slightly to the left passing to the left of a small pond then across boggy moorland (no clear path) to reach the unenclosed road of Stang Lane opposite the spoil heap and workings of Stang Mine.

4. Turn left down along the unenclosed road for 0.25 miles, with Shaw Beck on your right, then take the turning to the right along a farm lane (SP) that leads over a bridge across Shaw Beck then curves round to the left towards Shaw Farm, however, just after you have crossed a small bridge over a side-stream turn right along a rough track (do not continue to the farm) that leads quickly up to a gate in a wall just beyond a ford. Head through the gate then walk straight on alongside the wall on your left across two fields to reach a gate at the end of the walled fields (Seal Houses Moor ahead). Head straight on along the clear narrow path alongside the fence on your right (and the deep valley of Shaw Beck falling away to your left) and follow this on to soon reach the small side-valley of Gull Sike.

5. After this side-valley, continue alongside the fence across the grassy moorland then, after a while, the path very gradually bears away to the left from the fence and leads on to reach a gate in a fence across your path (path becomes a clearer track). Head through the gate then, after a few paces, bear off the track to the right along an indistinct narrow path passing immediately to the right of the stone-built shooting butt (closest to the track) and follow the path rising up across the rocky hillside. The path soon levels out and leads on above low rocky outcrops and boulders (High Eskeleth Farm

down to your left) then, just as the hillside begins to drop down into Arkengarthdale, follow the path curving round to the right down across the rocky hillside passing to the left of a small stone-built windbreak section of wall to reach the unenclosed road.

6. Turn right along the road and follow it on to reach a gate across the road just after a bench, after which carry on passing a farm on your left then rising up through the yard of the next farmhouse (hamlet of Seal Houses) and on passing some large barns then, just before the next farmhouse on your left, turn left through a squeeze-stile beside a gate (SP). Head straight on down across fields through four more squeeze-stiles and into woodland. Follow the path to the left through the trees then slanting down across Whaw Scars before bending sharply down to the right (above the rooftops of Whaw) to reach two stiles at the end of the woods. Continue down along the path to quickly reach the old Wesleyan Chapel where you turn sharp left over a ladder stile beside the row of cottages and down along the track passing Chapel Farm to reach the road beside Whaw Bridge.

7. Do not cross Whaw Bridge but head straight on along the track with Arkle Beck on your right (SP), through a gate passing a barn then follow the grassy track straight on across fields (Arkle Beck just across to your right) through a series of gates to join the wooded banks of the river. Continue straight on along the clear riverside path across meadows and through woodland for 1 mile until you reach a FB to your right just before the large stone-built Eskeleth Bridge across the river. Cross the FB then turn left along the riverside path to quickly reach the road beside Eskeleth Bridge.

8. At the road, head through the gate opposite to the right (SP) and follow the unenclosed track across the field passing a house on your left to reach a gate after which follow the track curving round to the left then turn right through a squeeze-stile just before the next house. Head across the field to quickly join a metalled lane in front of West House which you follow to the right across fields to reach the road just beyond St Mary's Church. Turn left back into Langthwaite.

MALHAM
Malhamdale

Malhamdale, as the upper reaches of Airedale are known, boasts some of the most spectacular scenery in England including Malham Cove and Gordale Scar, two of this country's great 'natural wonders'. These incredible natural landscapes attract over half a million visitors a year who come to admire the awe-inspiring limestone scenery on Malham's doorstep. The large car park soon fills up, with a constant stream of people following the boot-worn track to the foot of Malham Cove. Despite its popularity, it is an incredibly impressive sight. The best time to visit the Cove is on a warm summer's evening when the car park is empty and Malham becomes a quiet and dignified Dales village once again – and you will have the Cove all to yourself. The crystal clear waters of Malham Beck flow through the centre of Malham; in medieval times the beck divided the lands of Fountains Abbey to the west and Bolton Priory to the east. These monasteries controlled vast estates on the surrounding moors where they grazed their sheep, selling the wool throughout Europe. People have been living in this area since the Bronze Age as there are traces of hut circles on the surrounding hills, however, most interestingly are the clearly visible remains of field systems and ploughing terraces (lynchets) developed by successive waves of settlers including 8th Century Anglian farmers, Norsemen and medieval monks. Industry once thrived here with lead, copper, zinc ore and coal mined locally for centuries with its height between 1750 and 1860. The coal from Fountains Fell was used to refine lead and zinc ore at Malham Tarn Smelt Mill, the chimney of which remains.

THE VILLAGE

Malham is an attractive village and a popular base for exploring the surrounding 'limestone country'. It also lies along the Pennine Way and provides plenty of facilities for walkers including a National Park Information Centre, B&B's, cafés, village shop, outdoor shop, restaurant, Post Office, Youth Hostel, campsites and two pubs.

ACCOMMODATION

National Park Information Centre, Malham: 01969 652380

MALHAM PUBS

Buck Inn, Malham: **01729 830317**
This imposing stone-built hotel dates back to 1874 although it stands on the site of an older coaching inn. Inside, there is a comfortable lounge bar and dining room, however, after a day on the fells then the rather basic Hikers Bar is the perfect place to relax.

Lister Arms Hotel, Malham: **01729 830330**
Situated in the heart of the village overlooking the green, this former coaching inn dates back to the early 18th Century and was later named after its former owner Thomas Lister, who became the first Lord of Ribblesdale in 1797. The bar retains a great deal of character with many original features including an inglenook fireplace. Superb selection of Real Ales.

PUBS ON THE WALKS

Victoria Arms, Kirkby Malham: 01729 830499

Malham Walking Weekend
- Saturday Walk -
Malham, Janet's Foss, Gordale Scar,
Weets Top & Kirkby Malham.

WALK INFORMATION

Highlights	The Queen of the Fairies, a mighty chasm, wonderful views from Weets Top, a moorland cross, old tracks, a Saxon preaching cross and the watery grave.
Distance	8 miles Time 4 hours
Maps	OS Explorer OL2
Refreshments	Buck Inn, Lister Arms and tea rooms at Malham; Victoria Arms at Kirkby Malham.
Terrain	Clear field and woodland paths lead up to Janet's Foss, from where a quiet narrow walled lane climbs steeply up passing Gordale Scar before a rough walled track turns off to reach Weets Top (fine viewpoint). A clear path then a rough grassy track lead down across Hanlith Moor to join Windy Pike Lane (stony track) which is followed down into Hanlith then on to Kirkby Malham. A quiet lane heads steeply out of Kirkby Malham then field paths and a stony track lead back down into Malham.
Ascents	Weets Top - 414 metres above sea level Accraplatts - 300 metres above sea level
Caution	This walk climbs to Weets Top, which is exposed to the elements. The path across The Weets and Hanlith Moor is rough and boggy underfoot.

From Malham, a well-worn path leads alongside Gordale Beck, through some beautiful ancient woodland to reach the attractive waterfall of Janet's Foss set amongst rocks and overhanging trees. The word 'foss' is derived from the Old Norse word for a waterfall. This is a magical place, indeed, it is said to be the haunt of fairies where Janet (or Jennet), the Queen of the Fairies, lives in the cave behind the waterfall. The lime-rich water that tumbles over the waterfall has deposited a screen of tufa, a soft calcium carbonate deposit, on the mosses behind the falls to create a screen. The deep plunge pool at the foot of the waterfall was once used as a sheep-wash by local farmers to clean the fleeces before the sheep were sheared during late spring. The farm labourers would stand waist-deep in the icy cold water wrapped in sacking to keep them warm, with plenty of strong drink inside them as well! From the narrow lane above Janet's Foss, a clear path leads to Gordale Scar. No matter how many times you see this dramatic ravine it is always a "wow!" moment, with its towering crags, sheer scree slopes, jagged overhanging rocks, tumbling waterfalls and vertical cliffs over fifty metres high yet just ten metres wide. A footpath actually leads up through Gordale Scar, although this is only for agile walkers as it involves a scramble up rocks beside the waterfall. This huge cleft in the Mid Craven Fault is certainly impressive - the name 'Gordale' is derived from the Old Norse meaning an 'angular piece of land'. Views differ as to whether this was caused by glacial meltwaters or a collapsed cave, although it is probably a combination of both.

A vast tract of moorland known as The Weets rises to the east of Gordale Scar. A number of ancient tracks, as well as several parish boundaries, meet at its highest point known as Weets Top, with a weathered stone wayside cross marking this once important crossroads. There has been a cross here since medieval times, possibly erected by the monks of Fountains Abbey to mark the routes across the moors to their lands on Malham Moor and Mastiles. This is also one of the finest viewpoints in the Southern Dales with Simon's Seat, Barden Moor,

Flasby Fell and Pendle Hill clearly visible. An old track, walled for much of the way, leads down from the moor to the hamlet of Hanlith and on to reach Kirkby Malham.

The name 'kirkby' suggests that there may have been a Danish settlement and church here, indeed there is an 8th Century preaching cross in the churchyard. The Church of St Michael the Archangel is often referred to as the 'Cathedral of the Dales', a magnificent building that dates back to the 12th Century with 15th Century additions including the tower. It has a wealth of interesting features including a Norman font, the second heaviest bell in the country dated 1601 and also an invasion beam once used to secure the church door in times of attack from the marauding Scots. Cromwell is said to have signed the register as a witness to a marriage whilst staying with General Lambert at nearby Calton Hall. In the churchyard is the 'watery grave' that is divided by a stream. Separated by the oceans during their married life, Mrs Harrison thought it appropriate to be separated from her husband in death. When she died in 1890 she was buried on the south side of the stream, however, when they came to bury Mr Harrison ten years later they found the underlying rock on the north side to be too hard and so they are now united for eternity. Beside the church is the 17th Century vicarage, a wonderful three-storey house.

MALHAM SATURDAY WALK

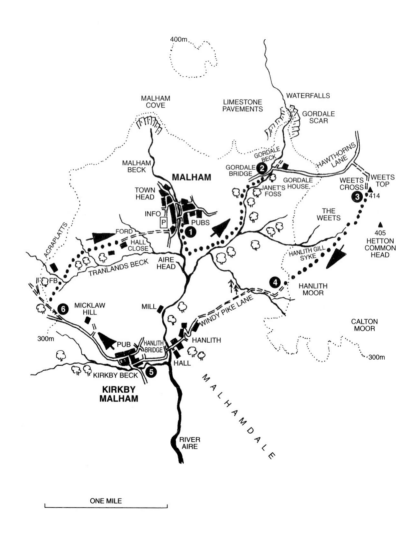

400m

MALHAM COVE

LIMESTONE PAVEMENTS

WATERFALLS

GORDALE SCAR

GORDALE BECK

MALHAM BECK

MALHAM

GORDALE BRIDGE ❷

HAWTHORNS LANE

TOWN HEAD

GORDALE HOUSE
JANET'S FOSS

WEETS CROSS

WEETS TOP

❸ 414

INFO
P
PUBS ❶

FORD
HALL CLOSE

THE WEETS

▲ 405 HETTON COMMON HEAD

ACRAPLATTS

TRANLANDS BECK

AIRE HEAD

HANLITH GILL SYKE

FB

MICKLAW HILL ❻

MILL

HANLITH MOOR ❹

300m

WINDY PIKE LANE

CALTON MOOR

300m

PUB
HANLITH BRIDGE

HANLITH

HALL

KIRKBY BECK ❺

KIRKBY MALHAM

M A L H A M D A L E

RIVER AIRE

ONE MILE

154

THE WALK

1. From the National Park car park, head left along the road into the centre of Malham passing the Buck Inn on your left then, where the road forks, follow the road to the right ('Gordale, Malham Tarn') over the bridge across Malham Beck immediately after which turn right along the track alongside the stream on your right. Follow this track down passing some houses on your left then, at the end of the track, head straight on along the streamside path down to reach a gate beside a ford on the edge of Malham. Head through the gate and follow the clear path across two fields, gradually bearing away from the stream, and through a kissing gate where you follow the clear path bending sharp left (SP 'Janet's Foss') passing to the left side of a barn. Follow this clear path straight on across meadows then alongside Gordale Beck on your right to reach woodland (National Trust sign 'Janet's Foss'). Follow the clear streamside path through woodland to reach Janet's Foss waterfall, where you carry on along the rocky path to the left of the waterfall up to quickly reach Gordale Lane.

2. Turn right along the road, over Gordale Bridge then follow the road bending round to the right passing the path to Gordale Scar *(detour to Gordale Scar - follow the clear path to the left to reach Gordale Scar after 0.25 miles. Re-trace your steps back to the road).* Continue up along the road passing Gordale House Farm on your left then follow the road climbing steadily up ('Dead End' sign) for about 0.75 miles then, where the road begins to level out at the top of the climb, turn right along a clear walled stony track (SP 'Weets Top'). Follow this track climbing steadily up to reach a gate at the end of the walled track (Weets Gate) beside Weets Cross with the open moorland of Calton Moor ahead.

3. Head through the gate and follow the right-hand path straight on (SP 'Calton') and follow this clear gravel path gently dropping down across the moorland then, after about 400 yards, take the grassy path

that branches off to the right (SP 'Hanlith') down to quickly reach a gate in the wall to your right. Head through the gate and follow the wide rough grassy path straight on alongside the wall on your left at first over an area of undulating ground at the head of Hanlith Gill Sike after which follow the rough grassy path gradually bearing to the right diagonally across the middle of the moorland (Hanlith Moor) to reach a gate in the far bottom right-hand corner of the moorland at the top of the walled track of Windy Pike Lane.

4. Head through the gate and follow this clear walled track straight on meandering gently down to reach the hamlet of Hanlith after 0.75 miles, where the track becomes a metalled lane. Follow this lane straight on winding steeply down through the hamlet to reach Hanlith Bridge across the Rive Aire at the bottom of the hill. Cross the bridge and follow the road straight on into Kirkby Malham to reach a T-junction with the main road beside the bridge across Kirkby Beck.

5. Cross over the main road along the lane opposite passing the Victoria Arms and then the Church on your right and follow the lane bending to the right around the old vicarage up to quickly join a road across your path. Turn left along this road (Cow Close Lane) and follow it climbing quite steeply up out of the village. Continue up along the road passing the turning towards Micklaw Hill, after which the road soon levels out then, where the road begins to rise up again, take the track that branches off to the right towards Acraplatts Farm over a stile beside a gate (SP 'Malham').

6. Follow this stony track straight on, over a cattle grid passing a small copse of woodland on your left then, just before you reach the woodland on your right, turn right over a wall-stile beside a gate (SP 'Malham'). Head straight down across the field to reach a wall-stile just to the right of a gate at the bottom, after which head straight on passing to the right of a ruined barn to reach a stile that leads over a stone slab FB across Tranlands Beck. After the stream, head up the small bank (SP) then walk straight on across the middle of the field (Acraplatts Farm across to your left) to reach a ladder stile, after

which bear very slightly to the right across the next field to reach another ladder stile between two gates. Cross this stile then head down alongside the wall on your right, through a gate beside a stone barn then follow the rough track bending round to the right around the barn alongside the wall on your right to reach a small wall-stile beside a gate (Weets Top directly ahead across the valley). Head through the gate then walk straight on down across the field along the indistinct grassy track, keeping fairly close to the wall on your right, to reach a stile beside a gate in the bottom corner of a field near to a stone house (Hall Close). Head over the stile and follow the grassy track straight on to quickly join a clear stony track beside Hall Close, which you follow straight on all the way down to reach the road beside the entrance to the National Park Centre car park at Malham.

Gordale Scar

Malham Walking Weekend
- Sunday Walk -
Malham, Malham Cove, Watlowes Valley, Nappa Cross & Pikedaw Hill

WALK INFORMATION

Highlights	The magnificent Malham Cove, a dry limestone valley, old monastic roads, a wayside cross to guide travellers, zinc mines and a superb descent along an old track.
Distance	5.5 miles Time 3 hours
Maps	OS Explorer OL2
Refreshments	Buck Inn, Lister Arms and tea rooms at Malham.
Terrain	Clear paths and tracks all the way. The climb up onto Malham Cove is very steep along a pitched-stone path. The path across the top of the Cove crosses limestone pavement with hidden holes. The path up through Watlowes Valley is rocky underfoot with a short but steep section. The remainder of this walk follows clear grassy / stony tracks across Kirkby Fell. This is open moorland, which is exposed to the elements. The descent follows a clear stony / grassy track all the way back to Malham, with some fairly steep sections.
Ascents:	Kirkby Fell (Nappa Cross) - 515 metres above sea level.
Caution	There is a steep climb to the top of Malham Cove, and care should be taken crossing the limestone pavement - keep well away from the edge of the Cove. The path through Watlowes dry valley is rough underfoot and steep in places. Do not explore the old mine workings on Kirkby Fell. Limestone is slippery when wet.

POINTS OF INTEREST

The reason people flock to Malham in their thousands is to see Malham Cove, for this is undoubtedly one of England's finest natural wonders. This incredible rock face is the result of huge movements in the earth's crust along the Mid Craven Fault millions of years ago which vertically displaced an immense slab of Great Scar Limestone over seventy metres upwards. It is truly an awe-inspiring spectacle; a huge natural crescent of rock towering into the heavens. The stream that bubbles up from the base of the Cove is not the stream that drains Malham Tarn, nor is it the source of the River Aire which rises from a large spring to the south of the village, but is actually a stream that disappears into a pothole near Smelt Mill Chimney to the north-west. Malham Cove is also famed for the superb limestone pavement that stretches across its top, created during the last Ice Age when ice movements stripped the vegetation away to reveal the pavement. This pavement consist of blocks of limestone, known as clints, with deep crevices in between known as grikes in which many rare flowers and plants shelter and thrive. When these ice flows began to melt, great torrents of water flowed across the uplands scouring out a deep valley above the Cove. These waters then poured over the lip of the Cove to create an incredible waterfall that would have dwarfed Niagara. As the ice melted and the ground warmed, this river found a new subterranean route thus leaving Watlowes valley 'high and dry'. This is a classic example of a dry limestone valley, indeed, the Malham area boasts the finest glaciated limestone landscape (known as glacio-karst) in England.

Several old tracks lead westwards from Malham over the moors to Settle and Ribblesdale. These routes were developed by monks during medieval times to reach their extensive lands and our walk takes advantage of two of them - Langscar Road and Stockdale Lane - passing the old monastic guidepost of Nappa Cross along the way. This simple stone wayside cross stands in its original base and is now set into a stone wall, although when it was originally erected to guide travellers across the hills there would have been no walls and few landmarks. There are fine views from Nappa Cross back towards Malham Tarn. Just beyond Nappa Cross, our route joins the old track of Stockdale Lane at Nappa Gate.

All around here are the remains of old mines, shafts and spoil heaps for this area was once mined for calamine, a zinc ore. Keep well away from the covered mine shaft beside the track just down from Nappa Gate for there is a vertical drop of 75-ft. The descent down along Stockdale Lane back into Malham is superb with Malhamdale spread out before you.

MALHAM SUNDAY WALK

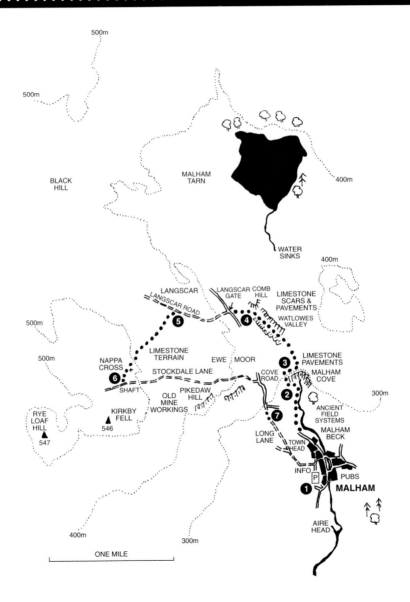

500m

500m

BLACK
HILL

MALHAM
TARN

400m

WATER
SINKS

400m

LANGSCAR
GATE

LANGSCAR COMB
HILL

LIMESTONE
SCARS &
PAVEMENTS

LANGSCAR ROAD

WATLOWES
VALLEY

5

4

500m

500m

NAPPA
CROSS

LIMESTONE
TERRAIN

EWE MOOR

LIMESTONE
PAVEMENTS

3

STOCKDALE LANE

COVE
ROAD

MALHAM
COVE

6

2

SHAFT

PIKEDAW
HILL

OLD
MINE
WORKINGS

300m

KIRKBY
FELL

7

ANCIENT
FIELD
SYSTEMS

RYE
LOAF
HILL

546

MALHAM
BECK

547

LONG
LANE

TOWN
HEAD

INFO

P

PUBS

1

MALHAM

AIRE
HEAD

400m

300m

ONE MILE

161

THE WALK

1. From the National Park car park, head left along the road into the centre of Malham passing the Buck Inn on your left then, where the road forks, follow the road to the left towards 'Malham Tarn, Arncliffe' and follow this straight on out of the village. After you have passed Town Head Farm, continue up along the road rising up then, after 200 yards, take the footpath to the right (SP 'Pennine Way') and follow the very clear path all the way to reach Malham Cove.

2. As you approach the Cove, follow the clear path which branches off to the left and follow this climbing steeply up a long flight of stone steps up the left-hand side of the Cove to reach the top. Turn right across the limestone pavement (take care - keep away from the edge) across the top of Malham Cove to reach a stone wall across your path just up from what was once the lip of the waterfall (with the dry limestone valley of Watlowes stretching away to your left).

3. Do not cross this wall but turn left and follow the clear path alongside the wall on your right heading up through the dry limestone valley of Watlowes to reach a double wall-stile across your path (National Trust sign 'Ewe Moor'). Cross the stile then continue straight on alongside the wall on your right heading up into the dry valley. The path gradually climbs up through this valley with the limestone crags closing in on either side then, as you reach the head of the valley, follow the stone-pitched path climbing steeply up to reach a stile at the head of the dry valley.

4. Cross the stile then continue straight on alongside the wall on your left for about 25 yards then turn left over a ladder stile (SP beyond the wall 'Langscar Gate') and follow the path straight on rising up alongside the wall on your right to reach a road by a cattle grid at Langscar Gate. At the road head through the gate directly opposite along a track, and follow this stony / grassy track straight on alongside the wall on your right at first then winding up across the hillside to soon re-join the wall on your right which you follow up to quickly reach a gate in a wall across your path (gate missing) where the track levels out for a while.

5. Head through this wall-gap, after which the track forks - follow the left-hand grassy track bearing round to the left up across the rough grassy moorland to reach a gate in a stone wall. Head through the gate and continue up along the grassy track bearing to the right through another two gates then follow the track bearing up to the left to join a wall on your left beside the remains of Nappa Cross set into this wall. Follow this wall straight on to soon reach a clear stony track across your path and a gate in the wall on your left (Kirkby Fell).

6. Turn left through the gate (SP 'Cove Road') and follow the clear track gently dropping down across Kirkby Fell *(danger - keep well away from the covered mine shaft on the left after a short distance)* with fine views across Malhamdale to reach a gate in a wall across your path after 0.75 miles. Head through the gate and follow the clear track winding more steeply down for a further 0.5 miles to reach Cove Road (enclosed by stone walls). Turn right down along the road for 0.25 miles and follow it dropping quite steeply down then, where the road bends sharp left, head through the gate on this bend to the right (SP 'Malham village').

7. Follow the grassy track straight on across the field to reach a gate at the start of a walled track. Follow this walled track straight on (Long Lane) to join a much clearer stony track across your path after 0.5 miles. Follow this clear track straight on passing Malham Water Treatment Works on your left and follow this straight on then bending left down to reach a T-junction with another track. Turn left along the clear stony track then, almost immediately (houses of Malham just ahead), turn right off this track along a rough walled path that leads down to join the road on the outskirts of Malham. Turn right back into the centre of the village.

MIDDLEHAM
Wensleydale & Coverdale

*Middleham is an elegant town of Georgian houses and older cottages
set around two market squares, behind which lie the ruins of a castle
with a fascinating history. Described as the 'Windsor of the North',
Middleham Castle dates back to 1190 and has played an important role
in the history of England as this was once the stronghold of the powerful
Neville family, Earls of Warwick, for over 200 years from where they
ruled their vast Northern estates virtually as a separate kingdom.
The heyday of the castle was during the 15th Century especially during
the War of the Roses. Richard Plantagenet, later the Duke of Gloucester
then Richard III, grew up at the castle where he later met his wife Lady
Anne Neville, the daughter of the Earl of Warwick - the Kingmaker. Their
son Edward, Prince of Wales was born at the castle. Richard became king in
1483 but was killed at the Battle of Bosworth in 1485. The castle soon fell
into disrepair and remained Crown property until 1625 when it passed into
private ownership. Much of the stonework was plundered in the 17th
Century, thanks to Cromwell's destructive tendencies. Middleham Church,
dedicated to St Mary and St Alkelda, dates back to the 13th Century,
although the site has been used for worship since Saxon times. St Alkelda
was a Saxon princess who was strangled by the Danes in the 9th Century
because of her faith. The remains of a Saxon woman, thought to be St
Alkelda, were found beneath the nave during restoration work in 1878.*

THE VILLAGE

Middleham is a delightful town where you will find a choice of B&B's, four pubs, public toilets, tea rooms, fish & chip shop, restaurant as well as a variety of shops including a small supermarket.

ACCOMMODATION

Tourist Information Centre, Leyburn: 01969 623069

MIDDLEHAM PUBS

White Swan, Middleham: **01969 622093**
A lovely old pub of great character with stone flagged floors, low beams, cosy corners and roaring open fires. This old coaching inn is said to date back to Tudor times.

Black Swan, Middleham: **01969 622221**
This historic 17th Century inn is situated beneath the ramparts of the castle. It retains the character, ambience and appearance of an old coaching inn with its stout stone walls, oak beams and roaring log fire set in a large stone fireplace.

Richard III Hotel, Middleham: **01969 623240**
Overlooking the cobbled market place, this three-storey 17th Century coaching inn backs onto Middleham Castle, indeed, the outer wall of the castle forms part of the restaurant.

Black Bull, Middleham: **01969 623669**
This corner pub is popular with the stable lads and jockeys from the many trainers in and around Middleham. Inside, there is a traditional bar with a flagged floor and open fire as well as a separate pool room.

PUBS ON THE WALKS

Coverbridge Inn: 01969 623250
Blue Lion, East Witton: 01969 624273

Middleham Walking Weekend
- Saturday Walk -
Middleham, Jervaulx Abbey,
Thornton Steward & the Coverbridge Inn.

WALK INFORMATION

Highlights   The legend of the Kelpie, the confluence of the Ure and Cover, monastic ruins, ancient bridges, a Saxon chapel and an ancient hostelry.

Distance   10.5 miles   Time   4.5 hours

Maps   OS Explorer OL30 & 302

Refreshments Pubs at Middleham and Cover Bridge. Tea rooms at Jervaulx Abbey.

Terrain   From Middleham, field paths quickly lead down to join the banks of the River Cover which is then followed to Cover Bridge from where a clear riverside path leads to the ruins of Jervaulx Abbey. A stony track heads across Jervaulx Park before a quiet country lane leads down over Kilgram Bridge. Field paths lead up through Thornton Steward then on to join a quiet lane near the Coverbridge Inn. Clear riverside paths and stony tracks head back to Middleham.

Ascents   No significant climbs

Caution   This walk crosses stepping stones across the River Cover, which may be difficult after heavy rain although an alternative route has been described. The banks of the River Cover to the west of the Coverbridge Inn are quite steep; take care after heavy rain.

POINTS OF INTEREST

The Cover Bridge Inn is an ancient hostelry situated adjacent to the narrow stone bridge across the River Cover. There has been an inn on this site for well over 400 years as the last Abbot of Jervaulx Abbey entrusted the landlord of the inn with the recipe for Wensleydale Cheese before he was sent to the gallows. The riverside path from the bridge to Jervaulx Abbey is an absolute delight passing the confluence of the River Ure and Cover, although be wary at dusk for this is the haunt of the legendary 'Kelpie'. From the turbulent waters this horse-like creature is said to rise to stalk its victims before pursuing them into the water. Jervaulx Abbey was founded in 1156 by a small group of Cistercian monks naming their abbey after the valley in which it lay, for 'Jervaulx' means 'Ure Valley' in Norman French. The monks chose remote locations for their abbeys where they could follow the strict rules of their Order - poverty, simplicity, spirituality and devotion to prayer. Their life was one of quiet meditation and prayer, leaving the manual work on their estates to the Lay Brothers who had taken the vows of the Order but had no study or choir duties; these Lay Brothers were the key to the success of the Cistercian Order. The abbey grew powerful and prosperous from sheep-rearing and horse-breeding; at one point nearly half of Wensleydale was in the hands of these entrepreneurial monks. But their most important gift to us came from their cheese-making skills for they produced a soft blue cheese, similar to Roquefort cheese of their native region of France, the recipe for which has remained in the area ever since and is now known as Wensleydale Cheese. They enjoyed quiet prosperity until the Dissolution of the Monasteries. There was huge hostility to this in the North of England, which led to the Pilgrimage of Grace in 1536. The last Abbot, Adam Sedbergh, was one of the leaders of this ill-fated uprising and was executed as a traitor in 1537. Thus Jervaulx fell directly to the King and its destruction was swift and ruthless. In 1600 the Jervaulx lands were granted to Sir Edward Bruce whose grandson became the first Earl of Ailesbury. The Abbey owes its preservation to the efforts of the Earl of Ailesbury who in 1805 ordered the ruins to be excavated and kept as a garden. The Jervaulx Estate is still one of the few privately owned Cistercian abbeys in the country.

Thornton Steward lies hidden away from the bustle of daily life, indeed the road through the village is a dead-end so it is always a quiet and peaceful place. Attractive stone cottage look out across a wide village green with the rolling hills of lower Wensleydale stretching away into the distance. A short distance from the village is the Church of St Oswald, said to be the oldest church in Wensleydale. This site has been a place of worship since pre-Conquest days, however, the present church is predominantly Norman built on the foundations of the Anglo-Saxon church, reputedly by Alan the Red of Britanny, Earl of Richmond and nephew of William the Conqueror, whose steward lived in the village - hence the name of Thornton Steward. Inside, there is a wealth of interesting features including Anglo-Scandinavian cross-heads and carved stones. Our route passes in front of Danby Hall, a fine well-proportioned house that is said to date back to at least the 14th Century, although much of the present façade is 19th Century. It has been the home of the influential Scrope family of Wensleydale for generations.

Ulshaw Bridge is a beautiful stone bridge with large abutments cutting into the mighty flow of the River Ure. This has been an important crossing point of the river since ancient times, indeed some historians suggest that it may even go back to Roman times. The present bridge dates from the early 15th Century when the Lord of Middleham gave money for its construction. This river crossing was an important meeting place in days gone by and a regular market was once held on the bridge.

MIDDLEHAM SATURDAY WALK

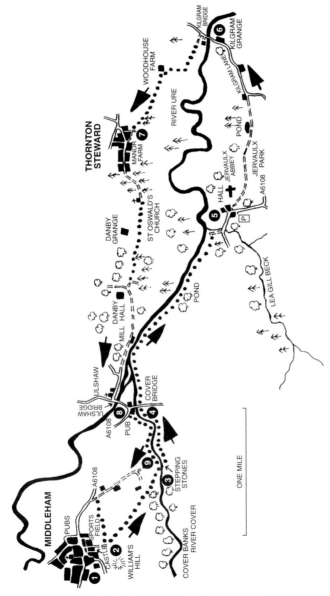

KILGRAM BRIDGE

6 KILGRAM GRANGE

KILGRAM LANE

WOODHOUSE FARM

RIVER URE

THORNTON STEWARD

7 MANOR FARM

POND

JERVAULX ABBEY

HALL

JERVAULX PARK

A6108

5

P

DANBY GRANGE

ST OSWALD'S CHURCH

LEA GILL BECK

DANBY HALL

MILL SHAW

POND

ULSHAW BRIDGE

8 PUB

A6108

COVER BRIDGE

4

ONE MILE

9

A6108

3 STEPPING STONES

MIDDLEHAM

PUBS

SPORTS FIELD

2 CASTLE

1

WILLIAM'S HILL

COVER BANKS

RIVER COVER

169

THE WALK

1. From the Market Cross in the centre of Middleham, head up along the Coverdale road that leaves the top of the Market Place passing the Black Swan on your left (signed 'Middleham Castle') and follow this road up to quickly reach the Swine Cross (weathered stone animal) and Water Fountain in the small market place known as the Swine Market. Turn left along the lane to quickly reach the entrance to Middleham Castle, just after which turn right along the track and follow this up (with the Castle on your right) to reach a gate at the top of the walled track (open field ahead).

2. After the gate, head diagonally to the left up across the middle of the field (SP 'Stepping Stones') along a wide grassy path then, as the field levels out, leave the grassy path and head more distinctly to the left across the field to reach a ladder stile beside a gate in the far corner of the field. Cross the ladder stile, then bear left down across the field and over a stile (in a small section of wall) then head to the right across the next field to reach another stile in the bottom corner just above the wooded Cover Banks above the river. Cross this stile and walk straight on along the top of this wooded bank then, as you reach a stone wall across your path, turn right down the steep bank to reach the stepping stones across the River Cover. *(If the river is in spate, turn left and follow the very clear riverside path with the river on your right all the way to reach the road near the Coverbridge Inn. Turn right along the road, over Cover Bridge, then take the path immediately to your left – continue on from Point 4).*

3. Cross the stepping stones then head through the gate just ahead to your left, after which turn left and follow the fence / wooded river bank to soon reach a stile across your path (SP 'Cover Bridge'). Cross the stile then head straight on along the top of a grassy bank on to reach the bottom left corner of a fence, just beyond which head to the right through a gate in this fence (waymarker). After the gate, turn left across the field, keeping close to the fence on your left, and through a small wall-gate after which follow the fence gently curving round to reach a stile beside a gate. Follow the path straight on with the river to your left then gently curving round to the right to reach the road at Cover Bridge.

4. Cross over the road (do not cross the bridge) and take the footpath directly opposite then follow this riverside path for 1.75 miles walking on a levee (passing the confluence of the rivers Ure and Cover) for most of the way until you reach a gate that leads onto a track. Head through the gate and follow the track up to the right away from the river to reach the road. Turn left along the road then, just after the road bends round to the right, turn left along the driveway towards Jervaulx Hall (SP). Follow this driveway on for a short distance then, where the metalled driveway bends to the left, follow the gravel track on curving to the right over a cattle grid (SP).

5. Follow this stony / grassy track straight on *(detour along the path to the left to Jervaulx Abbey – honesty box admission)* and follow it gently curving round to the left then straight on for almost a mile across the wooded pastures of Jervaulx Park, passing a large pond set amongst undulating hills, to eventually join Kilgram Lane beside an old gatehouse. Turn left along the quiet lane and follow it meandering down to reach the ancient stone structure of Kilgram Bridge.

6. Cross the bridge then follow the road on for a short distance passing the entrance to Yorkshire Water's 'Kilgram Bridge' treatment works just after which turn left along a track (SP). Walk along the grassy / stony track to soon reach a gate (open fields ahead), then head straight on bearing very slightly to the right across the field to a stile in the hedge on the other side of the field, then cross the next field to a gate in the top corner of the field. After this gate, turn sharp right heading up alongside the hedge on your right, over a stile beside a gate and up towards Woodhouse Farm. As you approach the buildings, bear to the left away from the hedge to reach a stile beside a gate (large barns ahead of you) then walk up across the next small field and through the left-hand gate (with the large barn directly ahead of you) that leads onto a farm track. Turn left

along this farm track through a gate and out onto open fields. Walk straight on across fields alongside the hedge on your left crossing two stiles beside gates then on to reach a stile over a fence by a small copse of woodland, after which bear up to the right towards Thornton Steward and through a small wall-gate in the hedge. Walk across the narrow field, over a stile then on through a gate to join a track where you head through the gate directly ahead and follow the enclosed grassy path straight on, which soon becomes a stony track which you follow bending up to the right into the centre of Thornton Steward.

7. Turn left along the road across the village green heading through the village to reach a gate at the entrance to Manor Farm. Head through the gate and follow the lane straight on passing Manor Farm then down through woodland to reach the St Oswald's Church, where you head straight on through the small gate out onto open fields. Continue straight on alongside the field boundary on your right through two more gates, after which cross a small drainage stream (Danby Grange Farm up to your right) and carry straight on with the wall now on your left through two metal gates across your path then passing a small copse of woodland on your left, just after which head through the gate in the wall on your left then head across the next field, keeping close to the wall on your right, to a gate in the top corner of the field (Danby Hall ahead of you). After the gate, turn left towards the Hall to soon join a track which you follow straight on towards the Hall to quickly reach a 'junction' of tracks beside a gate in the wall to your right. Turn left along this track and follow it heading across the wooded parkland (passing the Hall across to your right) down to reach a gate beside Danby Low Mill, where you follow the clear track straight on to reach the road. Turn left along the road to reach a junction just after the Catholic Church, where you turn left over Ulshaw Bridge to another road junction opposite the Coverbridge Inn.

8. Turn right along the road towards 'Middleham, Leyburn' for a few paces then turn left immediately after the house through a squeeze-

stile and follow the enclosed path down to quickly reach the banks of the River Cover. Follow this very clear riverside path along the wooded banks of the River Cover (river on your left) for 0.5 miles to reach a wall-stile that leads out onto an open field (end of the enclosed wooded riverside path). Carry straight on across the field, keeping close to the river on your left, to quickly reach a small gate through a tumbledown wall (with the stepping stones just beyond).

9. Do not head through this wall-gate but turn right up alongside the wall on your left heading up the short but steep bank then straight on across the field (still with the wall on your left) to reach a gate in the field corner beside a roofless ruined barn. Head through the gate and follow the enclosed path straight on, which soon joins a clear stony track. Follow this track to the right heading straight on for just under 0.5 miles then, about 75 yards before the track joins the main road, turn left through a squeeze-stile in the wall. Head up alongside the wall / fence on your right then, as you approach the top of the field, bear to the left (cutting off the top corner of the field) to reach a small wall-gate at the top of the field. After the wall-gate, head straight on (Sports Field to your right) to reach a kissing gate at the other end of the field that leads onto an enclosed path which you follow on to re-join the stony track near Middleham Castle. Turn right along this stony track passing the Castle back into Middleham.

Middleham Walking Weekend
- Sunday Walk -
Middleham, Hullo Bridge, East Witton & Cover Banks

WALK INFORMATION

Highlights	The legend of the buried treasure, racehorse gallops, a friendly bridge, Braithwaite Hall, a feudal village, two fine pubs and the wooded banks of the River Cover.
Distance	5.5 miles Time 2.5 hours
Maps	OS Explorer OL30 & 302
Refreshments	Pubs at Middleham, East Witton and Cover Bridge.
Terrain	This walk follows clear riverside and field paths all the way, with some stretches through woodland along the banks of the River Cover - this riverside path may be muddy after rain. The path 'down and up' Cover Banks is quite steep.
Ascents:	No significant climbs
Caution	The path along Cover Banks is undulating and rough underfoot, with some short but steep sections; take care after heavy rain.

POINTS OF INTEREST

Following the Norman Conquest, William the Conqueror gave Alan the Red of Brittany land in what is now North Yorkshire to subdue the unruly North. He built a stone fortress at Richmond and a wooden castle at Middleham on the ridge of land to the south of the present castle. The impressive earthworks of this early castle, known as William's Hill, can still be seen. Legend says that if you run round this hill seven times then an entrance will open to reveal a wealth of hidden treasure. Maybe there is some truth in this because in 1985 the Middleham Jewel was discovered in a field close by. This 15th Century pendant was sold for over £2.5 million in 1991 and is now housed in the Yorkshire Museum at York; there is a replica in the Castle Shop. The original castle was abandoned in 1180 when work began on the stone castle.

This walk heads up out of the town to reach the gallops of Middleham Low Moor, with the tree-shaded mound of William Hill across to your left. Whatever time of day you visit Middleham there always seems to be sleek racehorses either going up onto or returning from these gallops. Horse breeding and training can be traced back to the monks of Jervaulx Abbey, however, it was during the 18th Century that racehorse training began to flourish in this area. The growth in racehorse training brought prosperity to the town and it was not long before a racecourse was laid out on Middleham High Moor, with races being held until 1873. Middleham remains a major centre for racehorse training with over a dozen trainers and about 300 horses in the town.

A path leads down to reach Hullo Bridge across the River Cover, an old stone bridge set in an area of wonderful river scenery where the erosive powers of the water have cut a deep channel into the limestone bedrock. Just to the south of Hullo Bridge stands Braithwaite Hall, a fine example of a 17th Century hall with a distinctive roof of three pitched gables. The Hall retains many original features including wood panelling, fireplaces and an oak staircase and is now a working farm in the care of The National Trust.

Delightful field paths lead across Cover Banks to reach the attractive village of East Witton. The history of East Witton is closely linked to that of Jervaulx Abbey for it was the monks who planned the village we see today around its central green and developed it as a trading centre gaining a market charter in 1307. Following the Dissolution of the Monasteries the estate passed through various aristocratic hands, remaining essentially a feudal village estate well into the 20th Century. A fire swept through the village in 1796 destroying many of the thatched cottages and so the village was virtually rebuilt in the early part of the 19th Century on its old medieval foundations. The Blue Lion is named after the coat of arms of the Bruce family, owners of the Estate for many generations.

Swine Cross, Middleham

MIDDLEHAM SUNDAY WALK

MIDDLEHAM

PUBS

A6108

CASTLE

MIDDLEHAM
LOW
MOOR
(GALLOPS)

WILLIAM'S
HILL

MANOR
HOUSE
FARM

A6108

RIVER URE

COVER
BRIDGE

PUB

COLD KELDS BECK

RIVER
COVER

HULLO
BRIDGE

COVER BANKS

STEPPING
STONES

FB

EAST
WITTON
LODGE

RED
BECK
GILL

FORD

BRAITHWAITE
HALL

PUB

EAST
WITTON

200m

400m

BRAITHWAITE
MOOR

300m

400m

ONE MILE

177

THE WALK

1. From the Market Cross in the centre of Middleham, head up along the Coverdale road that leaves the top of the Market Place passing the Black Swan on your left (signed 'Middleham Castle') and follow this road up out of the town (take care) - the enclosed road soon opens out onto the gallops of Middleham Low Moor. Continue along the unenclosed road (with the gallops to your right) passing the entrance to Manor House Farm on the left after a short distance then, after a further 150 yards, take the path to the left (SP) through a wall gap. Head diagonally to the right across the field to reach another wall gap (just below the 'dog leg' in the wall), after which turn left and head down the hillside alongside the wall on your left to reach Hullo Bridge across the River Cover.

2. After the bridge, follow the footpath bearing to the left up the short but steep grassy bank to join a fence along the top of this bank - turn left along the top of the bank alongside the fence on your right. As you approach the stone wall ahead of you, cross the stile to your right beside a gate in the fence, then through the wall gate immediately ahead out onto a field. Bear to the right across this field to join a fence on your right that quickly leads to a FB over Red Beck Gill in the far right-hand corner of the field.

3. Cross the FB then head straight on alongside the fence / hedge on your right, cross over to the other side of the fence through a gap and continue on with the fence now on your left. Keep to this fence as it turns right then left around a 'dog leg' section to reach a gate at the end of the field. A clear track now leads straight on then, where this track bends to the right towards the barns, head left through a gate in the wall and turn immediately right alongside the wall along a grassy track. Follow this wall down (wall becomes a hedge in the next field) to reach a small plantation where you carry on along the field-edge passing the plantation on your right to reach a stile at the end of the plantation in the corner of the field. Cross the stile and

follow the clear path bearing to the left (keeping to the edge of the woodland) to reach a gate at the end of the woods, after which turn right along a grassy track.

4. Follow this track straight on, over a small ford then gradually bearing round to the right then, where the track turns sharp right, head straight on over the stile in the fence ahead of you. Head straight on through two wall gaps *(the second wall gap is just to the right of the small barn near a wall corner)* then head straight on alongside the fence on your right to reach a gate in the far right-hand corner of the field that leads onto the road (SP). Turn left along the road to emerge in East Witton at the top of the village green.

5. Head straight on down through the village then, halfway down the village green, turn left through a bridlegate immediately before the old Methodist Chapel (SP 'Cover Bridge'). Head straight on down across the field to reach a small gate in the bottom left-hand corner of the field, after which head straight on across the fields keeping the fence / wall on your right over a series of stiles, then take the FP to the right just before a barn (SP) through a wall gap. Follow the path skirting to the left behind the barn and over a stile beside a gate then walk straight across the field, through a gate and continue straight on bearing slightly to the right to reach a stile by another gate. The path heads straight on with the river to your left then gently curves round to the right to reach the road at Cover Bridge.

6. Turn left over the bridge and follow the road bending to the left passing the pub and then a house immediately after which turn left through a squeeze-stile and follow the enclosed path down to quickly reach the banks of the River Cover. Follow this very clear riverside path along the wooded banks of the River Cover (river on your left) for 0.5 miles to reach a wall-stile that leads out onto an open field (end of the enclosed wooded riverside path). Carry straight on across the field, keeping close to the river on your left, to quickly reach a small gate through a tumbledown wall and some stepping stones across the river just beyond.

7. Do not cross these stepping stones, but continue straight on along the riverside path through woodland. The path soon opens out into a small field - head straight on keeping close to the river to reach a small gate beside a large bend in the river, from where steps lead back up into the woodland. A very clear undulating path now threads its way across the wooded slopes of Cover Banks to reach a stile over a wall at the end of the woods, after which carry straight on across the open wooded pastures (with the river just to your left) to reach a stile across a stone wall with the river immediately on your left (waymarker indicating a sharp right turn).

8. Turn right after this stile and climb up to the top of the fairly steep bank then continue on, keeping close to the stone wall on your right, up across the wide field to reach a gate in the top right-hand corner of this field at the top of the wide ridge of land. Head through the gate and continue straight on, with the wall now on your left, heading down towards Middleham Castle. The path joins a lane through a gate which runs down passing to the right of the castle back into Middleham.

MUKER

Swaledale

Swaledale is perhaps the most beautiful and dramatic of all the Yorkshire Dales. The small villages and isolated farms of the upper dale are cradled by high mountains with evocative names such as Blea Barf, Rogan's Seat and Great Shunner Fell. Sparkling moorland streams cascade down the valley sides to swell the waters of the River Swale, England's fastest flowing river, which threads its way through a maze of fields dotted with stone barns. The finest hay-meadows in the Dales, arguably in England, can be found around Muker.

In spring and early summer the small fields along the flat valley floor are not the ubiquitous dark green of 'improved' fields but a mass of bright yellows, blues, reds and whites gently swaying in the breeze with over a dozen species of flowers such as buttercup, forget-me-not, cow parsley, clover, common bird's-foot trefoil and meadow cranesbill as well as an equal number of grasses. Cut later than normal to allow the wild flowers and grasses time to seed, these meadows are protected by law. Interestingly, the word 'muker' means 'meadows' in Old Norse, well-named indeed by the Viking settlers who came here over 1,000 years ago.

THE VILLAGE

Muker could be described as the perfect Dales village, a cluster of stone cottages set on a gently rising hill above Straw Beck with the tower of its 16th Century church rising above. It is a thriving place with a Post Office, tea rooms, shop, Swaledale Woollens, B&B's, campsite, toilets, craft shop and, of course, the Farmers Arms.

ACCOMMODATION

National Park Information Centre, Reeth: 01748 884059.

MUKER PUB

Farmers Arms, Muker: **01748 886297**
This warm and welcoming traditional village pub is situated in the heart of Muker. With its open fire, stone-flagged bar, cosy corners and hearty meals the Farmers Arms is the perfect place to spend an evening after a long day on the fells. The accommodation is self-catering.

PUBS ALONG THE WALKS

Kearton Country Hotel, Thwaite: 01748 886277

Muker Walking Weekend
- Saturday Walk -
Muker, Upper Swaledale, Kisdon Hill & Thwaite

WALK INFORMATION

Highlights	Glaciated valleys, fields of flowers, dramatic ravines, waterfalls everywhere, the Viking spring, an ancient corpse road, superlative views, wildlife photographers and old walled tracks.
Distance	8.5 miles Time 4 hours
Maps	OS Explorer OL30
Refreshments	Pubs at Muker and Thwaite. Tea Rooms at Muker, Keld and Thwaite.
Terrain	This walk predominantly follows clear stony / grassy tracks through Upper Swaledale with a number of fairly steep ascents and descents. The summit plateau of Kisdon Hill is exposed to the elements.
Ascents:	Beldi Hill - 370 metres above sea level Kisdon Hill - 490 metres above sea level
Caution:	This walk involves a number of ascents and descents, with a long a steady climb up onto Kisdon Hill, as well as several narrow paths across steep hillsides. When walking across the fields behind Muker, please walk in single file (hay meadows).

POINTS OF INTEREST

This walk encapsulates the Yorkshire Dales with hay meadows, riverside walks, field walls and barns, woodland, waterfalls, windswept summits and superlative views. Field-paths and stony tracks lead up through the deep U-shaped valley of Swaledale into a narrow wooded gorge near Keld with numerous waterfalls all around, in particular Catrake Force, Kisdon Force and East Stonesdale Force; 'keld' means 'springs' in Old Norse. This quiet village of old stone cottages and chapels seems to blend in perfectly with the surroundings hills, echoing the stark beauty of the landscape. To the south of Keld rises Kisdon Hill, which is surrounded on all sides by water with the Swale flowing to the north and east, Skeb Skeugh Beck to the west and Straw Beck to the south, indeed, it is sometimes referred to as Kisdon Island.

From the hamlet of Keld, our route follows a superb track up over Kisdon Hill with breath-taking views across Swaledale towards the high fells of Lovely Seat and Great Shunner Fell. The descent into Thwaite affords fine views across the deep valley of Swaledale. This track across Kisdon Hill once formed part of the ancient 'Corpse Way'. Before the church was built at Muker during the reign of Elizabeth I, mourners had to carry their deceased relatives to the nearest burial ground at Grinton, a journey that is believed to have stemmed from Norse mythology - it mirrored the journey of the soul from earth to the next life. The attractive village of Thwaite is famous as the birthplace of the Kearton brothers, pioneers of wildlife photography.

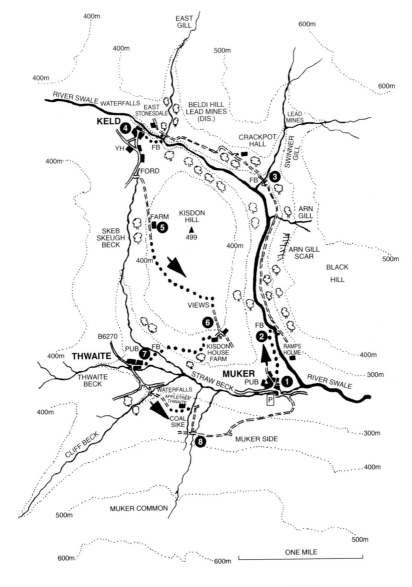

185

THE WALK

1. With your back to the Farmers Arms, turn left along the road then take the lane up to the left after a short distance passing the Literary Institute. At the top of the short bank the lane opens out into a small 'square' - follow the path ahead passing to the right of the small Post Office (SP 'Gunnerside and Keld'), through a squeeze-stile and out onto fields. Follow the clear paved path across a succession of fields until you reach the River Swale in front of you. Turn right to quickly reach Rampsholme Bridge (FB).

2. Cross the FB and up the steps ahead then follow the rough path to the left (SP 'Keld') which soon joins a clear, stony track. Turn left along this track and follow it heading up through Swaledale along the valley floor, with the river on your left. After about a mile, the track gently climbs up above the river, then drops down to reach a ford and FB beside a waterfall and some old lead mine buildings at the foot of the deep ravine of Swinner Gill (tributary of the Swale).

3. Cross the FB then head through the gate in the wall just ahead, after which follow the stony track winding steeply up at first then gradually slanting up across the wooded hillside (with the Swale down to your left). The track emerges from the woodland and levels out - continue along this clear stony track curving to the left around a barn then round to the right heading across the very steep hillside (steep wooded slopes to your left). After a gate, the track drops down to a bridge across East Gill, after which follow the path to the left (SP 'Pennine Way Keld') passing a waterfall on your left, to reach a FB across the river. Cross the bridge and follow the path steeply up to the right then, where this path reaches a wall and levels out, turn right along the enclosed path into Keld.

4. As you enter the small 'square', follow the road to the left up out of the village, bearing left at the fork in the road up to reach a junction with the main dale road (beside the War Memorial). Turn left along

this road for about 0.25 miles then take the walled stony track to the left (SP 'Muker') and follow this down over a ford. Continue along the enclosed stony track climbing steadily uphill to the right heading up across the steep flanks of Kisdon Hill and through a gate that leads out onto the open hillside - continue up along the track passing below an isolated farmhouse.

5. After the farmhouse, the track becomes a grassy track - continue straight on along this track gently rising up (with the valley down to your right), then follow the track as it bears slightly to the left through a gate in a wall (just to the left of some limestone crags). Follow the grassy track through a series of gates then out onto open moorland - carry straight on along the track across the top of Kisdon Hill to reach another gate after which follow the track down alongside the wall on your left then, after a short distance, bear to the right away from the wall along the grassy track dropping quite steeply down (views of Muker and Swaledale), then along a walled track at the bottom of the field that leads to a gate. Head through the gate and follow the walled track down then, after a short distance, the track opens out onto a field - head down alongside the wall on your right then, as you approach the bottom of the field (with the back of the farmhouse just ahead), turn right at the 'crossroads' of paths just beside a small barn (SP 'Pennine Way') and follow the enclosed grassy track on to reach Kisdon House Farm.

6. As you reach the lane beside the farmhouse, turn right through the wooden gate along a grassy track passing behind the farmhouse and follow this track alongside the wall on your left then follow the wall as it bends round to the left to reach a bridlegate. Head through the bridlegate, then walk alongside the wall on your right and follow it bending round to the right to reach a small wall-gate, after which follow the narrow path gently dropping down across the rough hillside to join a wall on your left (beside a small barn). Carry straight on alongside the wall on your left then, where it bends down to the left, head straight on along the narrow path gently dropping down across the rough hillside to reach a wall-gate (SP) beside another barn. Head through the wall-gate, then walk down the field

keeping close to the wall on your left then, at the bottom of the field, turn right to quickly reach an old bridge across Skeb Skeugh Beck. Cross the bridge then walk straight across the field, through a gate then bear slightly to the right to reach a squeeze-stile in the wall on your right just before the farm buildings. Head through the squeeze-stile and follow the enclosed path straight on passing to the side of a house to join a lane at Thwaite. Turn right along the lane and follow it to reach a road junction beside Kearton Country Hotel.

7. Turn left along the road, over the road-bridge and up out of Thwaite. Continue along the road passing the turning towards 'Hawes' (Buttertubs Pass road), 50 yards after which take the walled track that branches off to the right (SP). Follow this walled track on then, where it bends round to the right after a short distance, drop down off the track to the left through a small wall-gate that leads over a narrow stone FB across Cliff Beck above some waterfalls. After the bridge, head up across the field to quickly re-join the track (the track fords Cliff Beck just upstream of the bridge). Turn left along the track and follow it rising up across the field to reach a gate in the top corner, after which follow the track alongside the wall on your left passing the abandoned farm of Appletree Thwaite on your left then on passing a stone barn, after which the track becomes enclosed by walls for a short distance then opens out and leads across the small stream of Coal Sike to reach a gate in the bottom corner of the field. Immediately after the gate (with the barn in front of you) turn right up along the grassy walled track and follow this rising steadily up for 0.25 miles to reach a clear stony walled track across your path.

8. Turn left along this track then, after about 0.25 miles, the track forks – follow the left-hand track (clearer stony track) dropping steadily down across the hillside, with fine views across Upper Swaledale. After about 0.5 miles, the track bends down to the left and crosses a small stream at the bottom of the small 'valley' then rises up and bends to the left between two barns and leads on to join the road beside the bridge on the edge of Muker. Cross the bridge back into Muker.

Muker Walking Weekend
- Sunday Walk -
Muker, Oxnop Gill, Ivelet Bridge
& traditional haymeadows

WALK INFORMATION

Highlights	Hidden farmsteads, the beautiful wooded ravine of Oxnop Gill, a graceful arched packhorse bridge, coffin stones, riverside rambling and haymeadows.

Distance	4.5 miles	Time	2.5 hours

Maps	OS Explorer OL30
Refreshments	Farmers Arms and Tea Rooms at Muker.
Terrain	This walk predominantly follows clear paths across rough pastures and haymeadows through numerous squeeze-stiles, with a couple of fairly steep fields to cross. From Ivelet Bridge, the return section heads across flat haymeadows along the valley floor.
Ascents:	Oxnop Gill road - 335 metres above sea level
Caution:	When walking across the hay meadows do not pick any wild flowers or stray from the footpath - walk in single file. This walk involves a few short but steep ascents and descents across pastures.

POINTS OF INTEREST

From Muker, tracks and narrow paths meander across the lower flanks of Muker Common passing a cluster of old farmsteads at Rash, hidden away from the outside world. The views from this path are superb with the deep U-shaped valley of the Swale snaking away into the distance beyond the rooftops of Muker, with swathes of meadows punctuated by field barns and stone walls. This path leads up over into Oxnop Gill, a tributary of the Swale that cuts a deep cleft between the fells of Lovely Seat and Blea Barf, with the menacing sheer limestone crags of Oxnop Scar at its head, gleaming in the sunshine. Lower down, the steep slopes of this side-valley are thickly wooded whilst Oxnop Beck playfully tumbles over a series of small waterfalls before it drains into the Swale beside the magnificent Ivelet Bridge. This graceful arched packhorse bridge rises high above the river and stands as one of the finest bridges in the Yorkshire Dales. It is also steeped in history for this bridge was once on the route of the Corpse Way between the dale-head and the consecrated burial ground at Grinton. Coffin stones were placed at strategic places along this route on which the coffin could be rested, an example can be found beside the northern end of Ivelet Bridge. It is also said to be haunted by a headless black dog which will bring terrible misfortune if you are unlucky enough to see it!

A wonderful riverside path leads from Ivelet Bridge to Rampsholme Bridge, passing across fields of golden buttercups beside the wide stony riverbed of the Swale, England's fastest flowing river. The highlight of this walk are the meadows between Rampsholme Bridge and Muker, some of the finest traditional haymeadows in the country. These fields are a mass of yellows, blues, reds and whites with over a dozen species of flowers (I counted fourteen different flowers) and an equal number of grasses. They are protected by law, so please keep to the flagged stone path and, under no circumstances, pick any flowers. If you see anyone picking flowers, tell them off! Wild flowers look much better in a haymeadow that slowly dying in a vase on a mantelpiece! The best time to see these meadows is during May, June and early July.

MUKER SUNDAY WALK

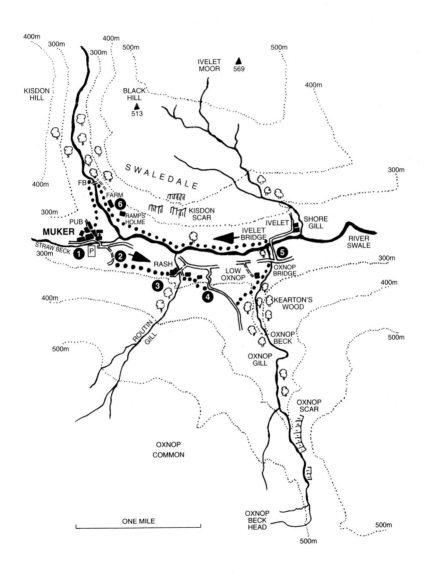

ONE MILE

THE WALK

1. With your back to the Farmers Arms, turn left along the road and follow this round to the right over the bridge across Straw Beck then bending sharp left just after which take the stony track which branches off to the right (SP 'Occupation Road'). Follow this enclosed track up through a gate beside a barn then continue on passing between a stone barn on either side of the track, after which follow the track bearing down to the right into the bottom of a small dip - at the bottom of this dip turn left through the second wooden gate in the stone wall.

2. After the gate, follow the clear narrow path straight on keeping close to the wall on your left, meandering across the undulating hillside across several fields to eventually reach a track and a black metal gate across your path just above a stone house (Rash).

3. Head through the gate and follow the track straight on to reach the next stone house after which continue along the track dropping down then, where the track bends sharply down to the left (SP) just after a small bridge, turn right through a gate and follow the track up to reach a large farmhouse set precariously on the hillside. As you reach the gates beside the house, turn right through a squeeze stile. After the stile, bear left across the field to a wooden stile after which head to the left alongside the wall and follow this up over another stile then on to quickly reach a squeeze stile beside a stone barn. At the barn (SP) head straight up across the field to reach a squeeze stile in the wall ahead, after which turn left, through a gate then on through another squeeze stile that leads onto the road.

4. Turn right up along the gently rising road then, where the road levels out, turn left through a gate (SP). Bear to the right down across the field to reach a squeeze stile in a stone wall immediately after the bottom end of the plantation on your right. After this stile, follow the field edge bearing round to the left (steep wooded banks of Oxnop Gill to your right) then steeply down a bank to reach a

squeeze stile in a stone wall just to the right of the large barns at Low Oxnop Farm. After the stile, bear to the right heading across the hillside (Oxnop Beck just down to your right) then across a meadow to reach the main road just to the left of Oxnop Bridge.

5. Turn right over the bridge then immediately left along a lane that leads down to Ivelet Bridge across the River Swale. After the bridge, turn left along the footpath (SP 'Muker') and follow the clear riverside path straight on for 1.5 miles across meadows and pastures to reach the houses at Ramps Holme.

6. Follow the clear path passing to the left in front of Ramps Holme Farm through a squeeze stile, then bear slightly to the right across the next field to reach a gate (beside a small barn), after which head straight on to reach Rampsholme Bridge just down to your left across the River Swale. Cross the FB then follow the path to the right (with the Swale on your right) for a short distance then turn left through a wall gate (SP 'Muker') and follow the clear flagged path across meadows all the way back to Muker.

Muker Church

PATELEY BRIDGE
Nidderdale

There has been a river crossing at Pateley Bridge for possibly 2,000 years as it is thought that the Romans came this way to their lead mines on the moors around Greenhow. Initially there was a ford across the river, however, a bridge was first recorded in 1320. Pateley Bridge grew in importance as it lay on the busy monastic road from Fountains Abbey over to Wharfedale as well as the old High Road to Craven. In the 18th and 19th Centuries a number of turnpike roads were established which, coupled with the local mines, quarries and mills, meant that the town soon became a bustling place. By the end of the 19th Century, Pateley Bridge supported two breweries and several pubs, most of which have now closed, indeed a closer look as you walk up the steep narrow High Street will reveal a number of old hostelries including the former King's Arms, a fine Georgian coaching inn, and also the ivy-clad Talbot Hotel.

THE VILLAGE

Pateley Bridge is a bustling Dales village, the 'capital of Nidderdale', where you will find a variety of shops including a Post Office, chemist, newsagent, restaurants, fish & chip shop, general stores, Britain's oldest sweet shop, craft & gift shops, the Playhouse theatre, Nidderdale Museum, toilets, car parks, recreation ground and campsite.

ACCOMMODATION

Tourist Information Centre, Pateley Bridge: 01423 711147

PATELEY BRIDGE PUBS

The Crown Inn, Pateley Bridge: **01423 712455**
At one time there were several pubs in Pateley Bridge serving beer from two local breweries, however, the Crown Inn is the only remaining 'proper' pub in the heart of this small Dales town. Dating back to 1767, it is situated on the steep High Street and boasts a non smoking dining room, lounge, bar and pool room - very much a traditional town pub.

Royal Oak, Pateley Bridge: **01423 711577**
Situated in Bridgehousegate, just across the historic bridge from Pateley Bridge, this traditional pub boasts two open fires, a comfortable lounge and bar area; note the original glazed tiling in the porch. Emphasis on home cooking with food served all day. No accommodation.

Harefield Hall Hotel, Pateley Bridge: **01423 711429**
This large country house hotel dates back to the 15th Century and once belonged to Bishop Benson, Bishop of Ripon, who used it as his country retreat before Henry VIII's Dissolution of the Monasteries. Set amongst 28 acres of grounds, this fine hotel boasts some more modern facilities including a gym, swimming pool, sauna, Jacuzzi and steam room.

PUBS ALONG THE WALKS

Bridge Inn, Foster Beck: 01423 711484
Ye Olde Oak Inn, Low Laithe   01423 780247

Pateley Bridge Walking Weekend
- Saturday Walk -
Pateley Bridge, Blazefield, Brimham Rocks, Smelthouses & the River Nidd

WALK INFORMATION

Highlights	The Panorama Walk, wonderful views across Nidderdale, hidden farms, ancient woodland, the weird weathered rocks of Brimham, a monks' trod, an old railway, imposing mills and the banks of the Nidd.
Distance	8 miles Time 6 hours
Maps	OS Explorer 298
Refreshments	Pubs, cafés and shops at Pateley Bridge; refreshments available at Brimham Rocks. Pub at Low Laithe.
Terrain	From Pateley Bridge, quiet country lanes and tracks lead high above the valley through Blazefield to reach White Houses. Paths then lead across fields and through woodland to join another track which is followed up to reach Brimham Rocks. After a short section of road walking, an old path (monks' trod) leads down through Smelthouses to reach the main road from where a riverside path leads all the way back along the banks of the Nidd.
Ascents:	Brimham Rocks - 260 metres above sea level
Caution	Take care when crossing the B6165 at Low Laithe. The path through Fell Beck woods is muddy underfoot.

In medieval times, the path known as the Panorama Walk was the main road between Pateley Bridge, Ripon and Fountains Abbey. Just after the cemetery, a walled path leads off this old highway to reach St Mary's Church. This lovely old church, now a roofless ruin, dates from the early 14th Century but was abandoned in the 19th Century as the town developed around the river crossing.

From Knott, a mixture of quiet lanes, tracks and paths lead down into the wooded side-valley of Fell Beck before rising up to reach Brimham Rocks. 300 million years ago rivers flowed over this landscape depositing silts which, over time, were compressed to form sedimentary rocks known as millstone grit. These rocks were exposed to the elements following the last Ice Age and since then have been ravaged by ice, wind and rain creating the rock masses we see today. Brimham Rocks have been a tourist attraction since the early 1800's, and many of the fanciful names given to the rocks were thought up by these early Victorian tourists. Brimham Rocks and the surrounding area was originally given to the monks of Fountains Abbey by Roger de Mowbray, as the Norman lords believed that such gifts secured a safe passage to the next life; the fine old track that leads from Brimham Rocks down to Low Wood House and Smelthouses was originally a monks' trod.

The final stretch of this walk follows the riverbank all the way back to Pateley Bridge, passing the old mill buildings at Glasshouses about mid-way. This riverside path follows the route of the former North Eastern Railway branch line from the Harrogate to Ripon line, which railway opened in 1862 and survived until 1964 - the old Station building can be seen along Nidd Walk. The railway crossed the bottom of the High Street by way of a level crossing and met up with the Nidd Valley Light Railway beyond Millfield Street, which was operated by Bradford Corporation between 1907 and 1936 to service the construction of the two huge dams in upper Nidderdale and also provided a passenger service as far as Lofthouse, the only rail passenger service operated by a municipality in the country.

PATELEY BRIDGE SATURDAY WALK

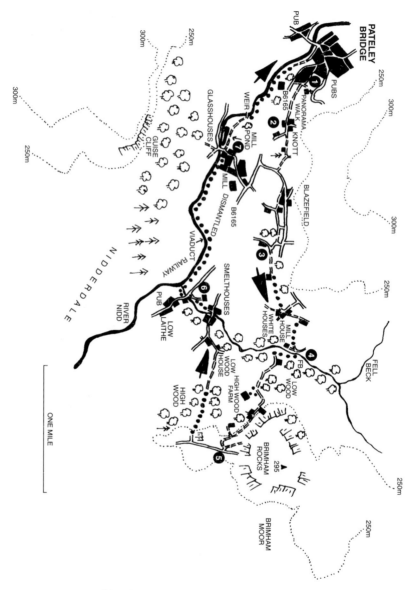

THE WALK

1. From the centre of Pateley Bridge walk up the High Street, at the top of which follow the main road round to the right (towards 'Harrogate') passing the Methodist Church just after which take the path to the left up some steps (SP 'Panorama Walk'). Follow this enclosed path climbing steadily up to reach the gates of the cemetery - follow the left-hand narrow lane straight on rising up then levelling out, with fine views of Nidderdale to your right, and follow this lane on to reach the group of houses at Knott.

2. Continue straight on along the road (SP 'Blazefield') then, where the road bends down to the right after a short distance, head straight on along the track that branches off to the left (SP 'Nidderdale Way'). Follow this walled track on to soon reach a house at the end of the clear track, at which point carry straight on along the enclosed overgrown path and follow this on, bearing right at the fork down to reach a road. Turn left up along the road then, as you reach the houses of Blazefield, take the track to the right immediately before the row of terraced cottages. Follow the clear track straight on passing in front of the cottages and houses keeping close to the wall / fields on your right (fine views across Nidderdale), and follow this on down to join a road. Turn left up along the road then, where it bends sharp left up towards the main road, head off to the right (on this bend) along an enclosed path (SP 'Nidderdale Way') which leads straight on to quickly join another road. Turn right and follow this steeply down then, as the road bends round to the right, turn left along a clear track (SP).

3. Follow this track straight on to reach some farm buildings where the track divides - follow the grassy track bearing very slightly up to the left passing to the left of the large barn, just after which the track forks again. Follow the left-hand track straight on between two stone gateposts then carry on along the clear path, with outcrops to your left, to reach a crossroads of tracks at White Houses. Head

straight on along the stony track (SP 'Ripon Road') passing in front of a house, after which it becomes a rougher enclosed grassy track which you follow on to reach a large house. Turn right along the enclosed path immediately before this house and follow this down over a stile, then head straight down the field over another stile across a fence then down to reach a squeeze-stile at the bottom of the narrow field. Cross the stile then head down alongside the wall on your left then turn left through a large gap in this wall and follow the clearly marked path slanting down across the hillside to join a track (Mill House across to your right). Turn left along this track to quickly reach a crossroads of tracks just after a cattle grid, where you head straight on bearing very slightly to the right down to quickly reach a FB across Fell Beck, set in woodland.

4. Cross the FB then turn immediately right alongside the stream on your right for a short distance then follow the clear narrow path meandering up through the trees to soon reach a junction of paths. Follow the path to the right (SP 'Smelthouses') to reach a stile at the end of the woods. Cross the stile and follow the enclosed path across the field to soon reach a rough walled grassy track, where you turn left up to reach Low Wood Farm. Head through the farmyard and follow the clear farm track straight on - continue along this track leaving the farm behind then bending up to the left through woodland *. The track soon opens out with a field on your left up to reach a gate across the track and the start of a walled lane - follow this clear lane straight on passing a scattering of farm buildings and houses then carry straight on (ignore any tracks off this main track) for a further 0.5 miles passing below the outcrops of Brimham Rocks to reach the entrance lane to Brimham Rocks (National Trust) where you turn right to quickly reach the road.

(on the OS map the footpath is shown as leaving the track as it bends up to the left through this woodland and heads to the right across the field towards High Wood Farm then, as the path approaches the farm, it doubles back to re-join the track about 25 yards further up - at the time of writing there was no sign of this path on the ground, so keep to the track).*

5. Turn right along the road and over the brow of a small hill, just after which turn right along a track (SP 'Smelthouses') and follow this on to quickly reach the right-hand gate of two gates (waymarker) beside some low outcrops. Follow the clear path straight on then down through High Wood - the path emerges from the woodland and continues straight on gently dropping down (Nidderdale ahead) and soon becomes a clear enclosed track that leads steadily down to reach a lane across your path opposite Low Wood House. Turn left along this lane down to join a road where you turn right into Smelthouses. Follow the road over the bridge across Fell Beck, just after which turn left along the driveway before the first house on your left and straight on over a stile then head on along the top of a low grassy bank (Fell Beck down to your left) and down through a gate at the end of the field. After the gate, bear slightly to the right through a squeeze-stile just ahead, after which walk alongside the wall on your left to join a track which you follow down, bearing left at the fork beside the house to quickly reach the main road.

6. Turn left along the road, over the bridge just after which take the path to the right (SP) and head down across the field to a stile in the bottom corner beside Fell Beck. A clear path leads over a small FB across this stream then left down to quickly reach the wooded banks of the River Nidd. Turn right and follow the clear riverside path heading upstream for 1.25 miles (passing below the old railway viaduct after 0.5 miles) to reach the old mill buildings at Glasshouses. Where the track opens out into a yard (mill building dated 1852) head left through the old mill yard to join the road, where you turn left then take the track to the right (SP) just before the road bridge across the River Nidd.

7. Follow this track straight on passing a large mill pond on your left and continue on (with the mill race on your right) to re-join the riverside again beside a large weir. Follow the track to the right passing an old iron bridge just after which you come to the end of the track and the start of the clear riverside path. Follow this clear riverside path heading upstream for 1 mile all the way back to Pateley Bridge.

Pateley Bridge Walking Weekend
- Sunday Walk -
Pateley Bridge, Providence Lead Mines, Ladies Riggs & Nidderdale

WALK INFORMATION

Highlights	The banks of the Nidd, a mighty waterwheel, the hidden tributary of Ashfoldside Beck, the scarred landscape of Providence Lead Mines, wild moorland and a fine walk across Ladies Riggs.
Distance	6.5 miles
Time	3 hours
Maps	OS Explorer 298
Refreshments	Pubs, cafés and shops at Pateley Bridge. The Bridge Inn beside Foster Beck (1 mile into the walk).
Terrain	Riverside paths then farm tracks lead up into the confines of Ashfoldside Beck. A clear track leads steadily up through this valley heading out onto the moors before a path drops steeply down over a ford across the stream before a path climbs steeply up across the mining debris of Providence Lead Mines to join another clear track. This track is followed down over Brandstone Beck then across Ladies Rigg (becomes a metalled lane) before dropping down to Pateley Bridge.
Ascents:	Providence Lead Mines - 280 metres above sea level
Caution:	This walk heads through an area of old lead mine workings with crumbling buildings, spoil heaps and shafts - keep to the path and do not explore the old workings. The ford across Ashfoldside Beck may be difficult after heavy rain.

POINTS OF INTEREST

The walk starts from the ancient bridge across the River Nidd from where a pleasant riverside walk takes us to the magnificent Foster Beck Flax Mill that dates from the late 18th Century, although it is said that the monks of Fountains Abbey built a small watermill on this site in medieval times. Nidderdale was once famous for linen weaving with over forty such mills between the upper reaches of the valley down as far as Knaresborough. The Foster Beck Mill was producing linen until 1967 and then it had a new lease of life for many years as the Watermill Inn, although it has recently been converted into apartments. The huge waterwheel dates from 1904 and remains in-situ. At around 34ft in diameter, it is one of the largest 'breast shot' waterwheels in the country capable of producing fifty horsepower. When the Watermill Inn closed, the pub 'transferred' to the old mill manager's house, which dates from 1878 and is now known as The Bridge Inn.

Old farm tracks lead up into the wooded confines of Ashfoldside Beck, as the upper reaches of Foster Beck are known, and a large caravan site hidden away from the outside world. The caravans are soon left behind as we head up into the hills, with the landscape becoming wilder with every step. Soon the old workings of the Providence Lead Mines come into view across the valley, and we follow a footpath down to reach the foot of the spoil heaps. Just beside the stream are the crumbling ruins of the former Smelt Mill with the collapsed remains of the flue climbing up the hillside. Above the scarred landscape of spoil heaps are the remains of the old Engine Shaft, with its conspicuous slender section of stone wall still standing. All around are rusting pieces of metal, decaying timbers from the mines and spoil heaps that have poisoned the ground so much that nothing grows. Lead has been mined in this area since Roman times, but it was during the medieval period that this mining became more organised. The land and minerals rights in this area were granted to Byland Abbey and Fountains Abbey in the 12th Century - Ashfoldside Beck formed the boundary between the two monasteries. Following the Dissolution of the

Monasteries, lead mining became much more sophisticated as companies and wealthy landowners began to exploit the mineral reserves on a larger scale; during the 19th Century this area was one of the most productive in the country. The mines closed around 100 years ago.

A superb track winds its way over into the neighbouring valley of Brandstone Beck before crossing Ladies Riggs from where there are wonderful views across Nidderdale - the final descent affords a bird's eye view of Pateley Bridge. Situated along the back lane through Bridgehousegate is a wonderful stone-built Victorian 'tower brewery' - ingredients go in at the top (water, malt, hops, yeast) and beer comes out at the bottom. A member of the Metcalfe family set this brewery up after a family row. Pateley Bridge's other brewery was located at the top of the High Street, established in 1775 by Elizabeth Metcalfe. Her brewery soon expanded to become a large commercial brewer known as 'The Nidderdale Brewery, J Metcalfe & Sons' that produced a range of fine ales until it closed in 1912, with most of the buildings later being demolished.

Brimham Rocks

PATELEY BRIDGE SUNDAY WALK

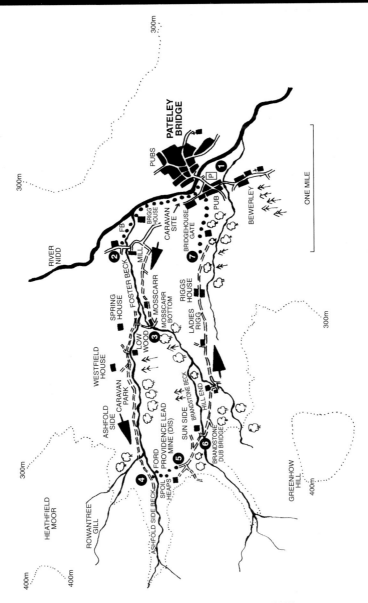

ONE MILE

THE WALK

1. From the bottom of the High Street in the centre of Pateley Bridge, cross the bridge over the Nidd then turn immediately right along the wooded riverside footpath (along the levee) across the Recreation Ground (bowling green to your left). The clear riverside path leads on through a caravan site then out onto open fields - continue along the now grassy riverside path then when you are parallel with Brigg House Farm across to your left the path divides - follow the left branch across the field to reach a kissing gate to the right of the farm buildings (beside Foster Beck). Head upstream then cross the FB beside the cottage, after which turn left alongside the stream then across a field to reach the road through a gate.

2. Turn left along the road, over a bridge passing the Bridge Inn and old watermill then continue along the road (take care) as it bends round to the right then, where the road turns sharp left, take the stony track to the right (SP). Follow this enclosed track bending to the left then sharp right heading across fields (ignore the left-hand branch heading uphill) all the way to reach the farm buildings at Mosscarr. Continue along the track passing between the bungalow and barns to reach the next farmhouse of Mosscarr Bottom. Head through the gates passing in front of this farmhouse, immediately after which turn right over a FB across Brandstone Beck.

3. After the FB head to the right up along the grassy track enclosed by walls then, where the walls open out as you reach the top of the bank above Ashfoldside Beck, head to the right down along a track and over a bridge across the stream that leads into Low Wood Caravan Park. After the bridge, head through the gate ahead onto a metalled lane across your path. Turn left along this lane heading up through the caravan park alongside the stream on your left (SP 'Ashfoldside Beck'). Keep to this clear lane, passing the ford / FB on your left that leads towards Low Wood Farm, after which the lane divides - head straight on (SP 'Nidderdale Way') to eventually emerge from the caravan site. Continue up along the lane, which soon becomes a stony track, heading through a series of gates up into the wild upper reaches of Ashfoldside Beck until you reach the conspicuous spoil heaps and old lead mine workings on the other side of the valley.

4. Take the narrow FP to the left (SP) off this track steeply down to a ford across the stream, after which head left passing the bottom of the flue and the old smelt mill buildings (crumbling building with an archway). Just after this building, follow the path to the right back on yourself (SP 'Nidderdale Way') slanting up across the hillside through the spoil heaps to reach a wall across your path on the far side of the spoil heaps. Follow this wall to the left uphill to reach a clear track at the top of the workings near to a conspicuous slender section of an old building (Providence Engine Shaft). Follow this track bearing round to the right then across moorland (barn across to your right) to reach a large gap (gate missing) in a wall.

5. Continue straight on along the much clearer track heading down alongside the wall on your right (SP 'Pateley Bridge, Toft Gate'), keeping to the clearer right-hand track at the fork ('Nidderdale Way'), down passing the entrance to Sun Side Farm to reach Brandstone Dub Bridge across Brandstone Beck.

6. After the bridge, continue along the track gently rising up to reach Hillend Farm, after which the track bends down to the right then curves round to the left over a small stream. The track now becomes a metalled lane which you follow straight on gradually climbing up across the wide ridge of Ladies Riggs passing an old roadside farm just before the highest point of the ridge. The lane then begins to gently drop down, passing Riggs House Farm on your right then, where the lane enters some woodland, take the FP to the left (way-marker post) through the trees to quickly reach a stile in the corner.

7. After the stile, head to the right down alongside the field boundary to reach a small gate in the bottom corner. After this gate, continue straight on down to join a track that leads between the houses to reach the road in Bridgehousegate opposite the Old Brewery. Turn right along the road then take the path to the left after the parking area that leads back to the Recreation Ground.

REETH

Swaledale

Reeth is a delightful small Dales' town, the 'capital of Swaledale', with elegant Georgian houses, old stone cottages and ancient inns overlooking a large sloping green where weekly markets are still held on the cobbled verges. All around are the high fells of Swaledale, with the dramatic scars and screes of Fremington Edge dominating the scene and Calver Hill rising up behind the village to a height of 487 metres; this village can almost be described as perfect. Reeth developed as a trading centre near to the confluence of Arkle Beck and the River Swale, however, its main period of growth was during the 18th and 19th centuries when the village became a centre for the local lead mining and hand knitting industries as well as farming. Reeth gained its market charter in the late 17th Century and soon boasted seven annual fairs, a weekly market and a population three times greater than that of today during the mining heyday of the early 19th Century. However, by the end of the 19th Century the mines had closed and many people left to look for work in Lancashire or the North East. The surrounding hills and moors are littered with a fascinating legacy from the past 3,000 years of human history with prehistoric earthworks, Bronze Age forts, extensive lead mine remains, old farmhouses and ancient tracks.

THE VILLAGE

Reeth is an ideal base from where to explore the surrounding hills as it boasts an abundance of cafés, pubs and shops as well as a choice of three great pubs. There is also a National Park Information Centre, Swaledale Folk Museum, Post Office, general stores, bakery, craft shops, hotel, bookshop, newsagent, garage, travelling fish & chip van (Fridays), toilets, telephone and campsite.

ACCOMMODATION

National Park Information Centre, Reeth: 01748 884059.

REETH PUBS

The Buck Hotel, Reeth: **01748 884210**
This imposing old coaching inn looks out across the large sloping green, situated beside the Arkengarthdale road. Inside, the large comfortable bar is warmed by an open fire.

The Kings Arms, Reeth: **01748 884259**
This wonderful old Georgian inn is known locally as the 'middle house'. Inside, it boasts one of the finest inglenook fireplaces in the Dales whilst outside you can enjoy a quiet pint sat around a table on the old marketplace cobblestones.

The Black Bull, Reeth: **01748 884213**
This historic inn is a prominent local landmark with its three-storey whitewashed façade. The pub retains a great deal of character with slanting doorways, stone-flagged floor, low beams and a large open fireplace. The bow-fronted window of the restaurant once belonged to a Georgian drapers shop. Note the upside down sign - the result of a long running planning dispute with the National Park Authority.

PUBS ALONG THE WALKS

Bridge Inn, Grinton   01748 884224

Reeth Walking Weekend
- Saturday Walk -
Reeth, Apedale, High Carl
& Swaledale

WALK INFORMATION

Highlights   Abandoned lead mines, great views from Greets Hill, the valley of the apes, an old road over to Swaledale, superlative views, old miners' tracks and a swaying bridge across the Swale.

Distance   11 miles   Time   5 hours

Maps   OS Explorer OL30

Refreshments   Pubs, cafés and shops at Reeth. Pub at Grinton. No facilities along this route - take provisions with you.

Terrain   This walk heads through remote countryside climbing up onto the exposed moorland of Greets Hill and High Carl at the head of Apedale. This walk predominantly follows stony tracks, which makes route-finding relatively easy, although there are one or two sections along indistinct paths across heather moorland. Choose a clear day as the views from High Carl across Swaledale are superb.

Ascents: Greets Hill - 508 metres above sea level
High Carl - 550 metres above sea level

Caution: This walk heads through remote countryside along old stony tracks or moorland paths. Navigation may be difficult in poor weather. The ascents and descents are long and steady.

POINTS OF INTEREST

This walk is one of the finest moorland treks in the Yorkshire Dales, with old miners' trods and shooters' tracks underfoot for almost the entire walk. The decaying remains of lead mines and spoil heaps are a constant companion along this route, although the most memorable aspects are the views. The initial climb from Grinton up onto the summit of Greets Hill affords wonderful views back towards Reeth with its large sloping green set on the lower flanks of Calver Hill and the gleaming limestone scars of Fremington Edge towering above. Greets Hill is the highest ground between the Yorkshire Dales and North York Moor and as such provides a vast panorama across much of North Yorkshire with the industrial sprawl of Teesside clearly visible on the horizon, whilst to the south lies Wensleydale.

A fine shooters' track leads down into Apedale, a remote and lonely valley hidden away amongst the hills between Swaledale and Wensleydale. This desolate valley lies in the shadow of Gibbon Hill, however, this was not once the preserve of our hairy cousins but was first settled by 'Appi' a Viking chieftain over 1,000 years ago! Our route follows an old track known as Apedale Road climbing gradually up to the head of Apedale passing through an area scarred with old lead mines. Swaledale was once a major centre for lead mining, indeed lead has been mined in this area since at least Roman times, however its heyday was during the 19th Century when levels were driven deep into the hillsides, large smelting mills were built in the many side-valleys and miners' cottages swamped former farming villages; the crumbling remains of this long forgotten industry can be seen throughout this walk. A final short but steep climbs takes us up onto the watershed on the upper flanks of High Carl before a gradual descent through an area littered with old spoil heaps then across Whitaside Moor down to Harkerside Place Farm - with fine views across Swaledale all around. The final section back to Reeth crosses the Swing Bridge over the Swale, which was re-built in 2002 after it had been washed away in floods two years earlier; the Swale is said to be the fastest flowing river in England and can rise an amazing three metres in 20 minutes.

REETH SATURDAY WALK

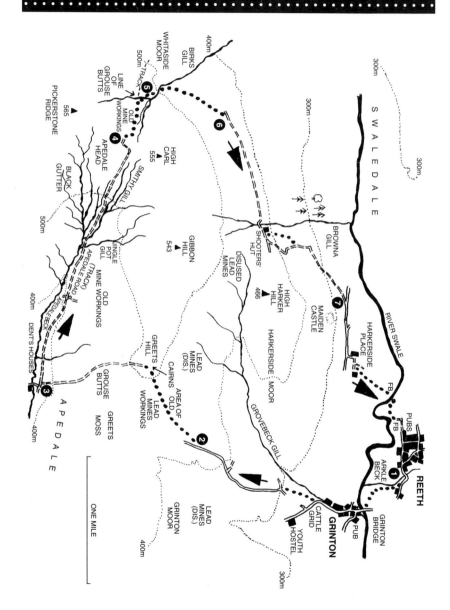

THE WALK

1. Leave Reeth along the 'Richmond' road and follow this road down out of the bottom corner of the large green, then round to reach Reeth Bridge across Arkle Beck. Cross the bridge and follow the road round to the right (with Arkle Beck on your right) then take the path to the right (SP 'Grinton') just before you enter Fremington. Follow this clear path alongside Arkle Beck passing farm buildings and the remains of Fremington Mill on your left then follow the clear path straight on across the field to join a corner of a stone wall on your left (SP) and follow this round to the left, through a kissing gate then straight on up some steps onto Grinton Bridge across the River Swale. Turn right along the road over the bridge then, where the main road bends sharp left, head straight on along the road (road sign 'Redmire, Leyburn') heading up the hill through the village until you reach a cattle grid across the road (unfenced road and open moorland ahead). Take the path to the right through a small gate immediately before this cattle grid (SP) and follow the unclear path straight up the heather-covered hillside (no clear path) bearing very slightly to the left until a sharp bend in the unfenced moorland road (marked by a triangular road sign) becomes visible; head up to join the road on this sharp bend. Follow this unfenced road climbing steadily uphill for approx. 0.75 miles (ignore tracks to your right marked 'Bridleway only - no vehicles) then, where the road levels out, continue along the unfenced road for a further 0.25 miles then take the bridleway which branches off to the right away from the road (SP).

2. Follow the wide grassy path bearing slightly to the right (away from the road) heading up across the hillside through an area of old mining spoil heaps (path marked by cairns) up to reach the two prominent cairns on the summit of Greets Hill. Continue along the path passing these two cairns to quickly reach a gate in a fence across your path at the top of the hill. Head through the gate then carry straight on to quickly join a clear shooter's track which you follow

straight on dropping down into Apedale for approx. 1 mile to reach a junction of tracks at the bottom of the valley (just up from the stone bridge across Apedale Beck and the stone-built shooters' hut).

3. Turn right along the track heading up into Apedale (with Apedale Beck just down to your left) - follow this clear stony track (Apedale Road) straight on for about 2 miles heading gradually up into the valley (ignore the track branching down to the left just after the old mine workings). As you reach the head of the valley, continue along the stony track climbing steeply up before levelling out passing an old railway wagon then climbing up again (track becomes much rougher underfoot) up onto the top of the moorland. As you approach the fence-line across your path follow the rough track bending sharply to the left (large cairn) then round to the right to a gate in this fence at the top of the pass.

4. Head through the gate and follow the wide rough track straight on then bending to the right after a short distance then round to the left (cairns) - follow this wide rough track straight on dropping down (Swaledale in the distance) through an area of old mining debris. After about a quarter of a mile you cross a line of shooting butts - turn right here off the track passing shooting butt number 10.

5. Follow the shooting butts down (indistinct path - boggy in places) then cross over the small stream of Birks Gill (just after shooting butt number 6) after which the path becomes clearer heading down alongside this stream then, as you approach shooting butt number 3 follow the clear narrow path bearing to the right across the flanks of High Carl. Follow this clear path straight on across the heather-clad Whitaside Moor (superb views of Swaledale to your left) to eventually join a stony shooters' track on your left.

6. Head straight on (to the right) along this shooters' track and follow it across the upper flanks of High Carl and Gibbon Hill (Swaledale down to your left) - keep to this clear stony track heading straight on to reach a large wooden shooters' hut after about a mile. Turn left

down off the track immediately after this wooden shooters' hut (no clear path) bearing very slightly to the right down across the steep rough hillside to join a rough grassy path across your path (where the hillside levels out slightly). Turn right along this rough path to quickly join a clear stony track coming down the hillside, which you follow to the left winding all the way down to reach the road.

7. Turn right along the road for 0.5 miles to reach the entrance to Harkerside Place Farm (SP 'Reeth via Swing Bridge').Turn left down along the stony track towards the farm, over a cattle grid and into the farmyard - as you enter the farmyard take the first turning to the right along a clear farm track (SP). Follow this track on then, where the track forks after about 200 yards, head to the left through a gate in the wall just before another stone farmhouse (SP 'Grinton Swing Bridge'). Bear to the right down across the field (do not head along the stony track) through a small wall-gate, after which head diagonally down across the field through another wall-gate then down to reach the large Suspension Bridge over the River Swale. Cross the bridge, turn right and follow the clear path across fields then, as you reach a large meander in the river, head over a small FB over boggy ground then follow the clear enclosed path up to the left to join the end of a lane which you follow to the right into Reeth.

Reeth Walking Weekend
- Sunday Walk -
Reeth, Marrick Priory
& the Nuns' Causey

Highlights   The end of the Corpse Way, ancient earthworks and monastic remains, a nuns' staircase, England's fastest flowing river, a hill-top village and superb views.

Distance   6 miles   Time   2.5 hours

Maps   OS Explorer OL30

Refreshments: Pubs, cafés and shops at Reeth or the Bridge Inn at Grinton.

Terrain   From Reeth, riverside paths and then field paths lead to Marrick Abbey, from where there is a steep climb up through Steps Wood to the village of Marrick. After a short section of road walking, a path cuts across Reels Head (superb views) before dropping steeply down a quiet lane then across fields to reach High Fremington and back to Reeth.

Ascents: Reels Head - 330 metres above sea level

Caution: This walk involves a fairly steep climb up through Steps Wood along an old paved trod (slippery when wet). Take care when walking along the quiet country lanes around Marrick and Reels Head.

POINTS OF INTEREST

From the picturesque village of Reeth, 'capital of Swaledale', pleasant field paths take us past an old mill that still retains its waterwheel to reach Grinton Bridge. The Church of St Andrew dominates the village of Grinton and is affectionately known as the 'Cathedral of the Dales'. It has served as a place of worship for over 1,000 years originally for pagan ceremonies, later being adopted by the Christian church. Parts of the original Norman church survive although much of the present day church dates from the 14th to 16th centuries. The parish of Grinton once stretched the entire length of Swaledale as far as the old Westmorland boundary making it the largest parish in Yorkshire. For centuries the people of Upper Swaledale had to carry their dead along a 12-mile track known as the 'Corpse Way' for burial at Grinton. This journey originally stemmed from Norse mythology in which the 'Corpse Way' mirrored the final passage of the soul from earth to the next life. Thankfully for the people of the upper dale a church was built at Muker in 1580.

A delightful riverside path takes us down along the banks of the River Swale with glimpses of Marrick Priory's tower in the distance. Note the strange earthworks on the opposite bank, which are the remains of defensive ramparts and ditches built almost 2,000 years ago by the native Brigantes tribes to defend their lands against the advancing Roman legions. We soon come to the hamlet of Marrick Abbey and the remains of Marrick Priory, with its large tower rising high above the valley floor beside the River Swale. This Benedictine priory was founded in 1154 by Robert de Aske for a small community of nuns. Unlike many other priories and abbeys, Marrick did not accrue vast estates of land and wealth and only had twelve nuns at the time of its Dissolution under the orders of Henry VIII in 1539, after which the buildings were used as the Parish church for Marrick and more recently as an outdoor centre and farm. According to local legend a tunnel once connected Marrick Priory with Ellerton Priory, a Cistercian Priory just across the river, thus enabling the nuns to visit each other in secret! A series of old stone steps, known as the 'Nuns' Causey', still links Marrick Priory with the village of Marrick perched 300 metres up on the hillside. Marrick enjoys an elevated and windswept position high above the valley, its old farms and cottages interspersed with fields; it is difficult to imagine the hive of industrial activity that once took place in this area when the whole swathe of land from Marrick to Hurst and beyond was a centre for lead mining. Years ago Marrick boasted an inn called the White Horse, a schoolhouse and chapel, all of which have now closed. From Marrick, the moorland road is followed for a short distance before a footpath cuts off across the hillside over to Reels Head. As you walk over the rise of the hill, a superb view of Swaledale begins to unfold in front of you with the houses of Reeth set beneath the slopes of Calver Hill and the deep valley curving away into the distance. It is one of those 'wow!' viewpoints that makes you just stop and stare.

Reeth

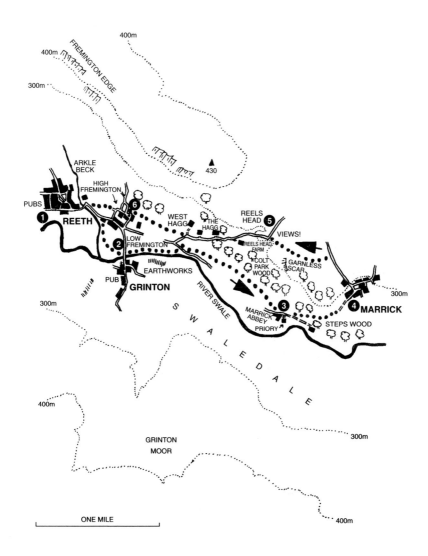

THE WALK

1. Leave Reeth along the 'Richmond' road and follow this down out of the bottom corner of the large green, then round to reach Reeth Bridge across Arkle Beck. Cross the bridge and follow the road round to the right (with Arkle Beck on your right) then take the footpath to the right (SP 'Grinton') just before you enter Fremington. Follow this clear path alongside Arkle Beck passing farm buildings and the remains of Fremington Mill on your left then follow the clear path straight on across the field (passing a solitary tree) to join a corner of a stone wall on your left (SP) and follow this round to the left, through a kissing gate then straight on up some steps onto Grinton Bridge across the River Swale.

2. At the road (on Grinton Bridge), turn left then right immediately after the bridge down along a track to join a riverside path (SP). Follow this clear path straight on alongside the River Swale over a number of stiles to eventually climb up the wooded riverbank to reach a road. Turn left along the road then, after a short distance, take the footpath to the right over a stile, after which bear right across the field gradually gaining height to reach a stile over a fence, cross the stile and continue straight on through a small wooden gate (Colt Park Wood up to your left). Follow the path ahead through a series of wall gaps and stiles (with the tower of Marrick Priory in the distance) eventually dropping down to reach the road at Marrick Abbey through a gate in the bottom right hand corner of the field.

3. Turn left along the road passing the farm and Priory buildings on your right, continue along the road over a cattle grid after which take the path to the left (SP 'Marrick'). Head up the grassy track to the right and through a gate that leads into Steps Wood. Follow the stone steps climbing up through the wood to reach a gate at the top of the steps / woods then continue straight on up alongside the stone wall on your right to join a track by a barn, which you follow straight on into Marrick.

4. Follow the metalled lane, passing the old Methodist Chapel, into the village and take the first turning on the left after the 'Old Blacksmiths Shop' up to reach a road junction beside a small triangular 'green' with a wooden seat. Head straight on to the left up along the road out of the village passing a farm on your left. The road soon levels out then gradually drops down into a small dip - take the footpath to the left (SP) through a small wall-gate. Head up across the field alongside the stone wall on your right then, as you near the top of the field and a gate across your path, head through a squeeze-stile through the wall to the right. After the squeeze-stile turn left heading up with the stone wall now on your left - follow this wall all the way to reach the road at Reels Head (superb views of Reeth and Swaledale ahead).

5. At the road, turn left and follow it winding quite steeply down the 1-in-6 hill (take care) passing the entrance to The Hagg farm. Continue along the road as it begins to level out then, just after the entrance to West Hagg Farm where the road bends round to the left, take the footpath to the right (SP 'Fremington'). Head to the left across the field to reach a squeeze-stile in the corner of the stone wall, after which head straight on alongside the stone wall on your right to reach a small gate beside a larger gate just after the wall has gently curved round to the right. Head through this gate and continue straight on with the stone wall now on your left to reach an old enclosed grassy track above Sorrel Sykes Farm. Head over this track along the clear path alongside the stone wall on your right, which soon becomes an enclosed path that leads on to join a narrow road at High Fremington.

6. Turn left along the road to quickly reach a junction where you turn right then, where the road bends down to the left, head straight on along a track through a gate (SP). Head straight on forsaking the track for the grassy path alongside the wall on your left that leads down through a squeeze-stile then on across a field to join the road beside Reeth Bridge. Cross the bridge back up into Reeth.

For an alternative walk from Reeth please see Walking Weekend 9

WEST BURTON

Bishopdale

*West Burton is proclaimed by many to be the most beautiful
village in England and it is easy to see why; the hills of Bishopdale
look down upon an idyllic scene of village green, stone cottages,
country inn and stream complete with a waterfall. The village stands
at the confluence of Bishopdale and the Walden valley, which is
somewhat of a rarity in the Yorkshire Dales as it does not have the
suffix 'dale'. This remote and hidden valley was the last refuge of the
Celtic tribes fleeing the invading Angles, Saxons and Norsemen,
indeed 'Walden' means 'Valley of the Welsh' as these native tribes
British were known. Out of the bottom corner of the green,
a track leads down to West Burton Falls, also known as Couldron
Force, which have a delightful setting amongst rocks and
overhanging trees where the waters of Walden Beck cascade over
rock ledges into a deep pool.*

THE VILLAGE

The highlight of West Burton is its large village green surrounded by old stone houses and the ever-watching fells rising steeply above. Here you will find B&B's, a village shop and Post Office, butcher's shop, craft shop, bus service and the Fox & Hounds Inn.

ACCOMMODATION

National Park Information Centre, Aysgarth Falls: 01969 662910

WEST BURTON PUB

Fox & Hounds, West Burton: **01969 663111**
Traditional village 'local' offering good Yorkshire ales, roaring fires and a buzzing atmosphere - a great place to enjoy a pint at the end of these walks. The sprawling village green also doubles as a vast beer garden in summer.

PUBS ALONG THE WALKS

Foresters Arms, Carlton:	01969 640272
Wensleydale Heifer, West Witton:	01969 622322
Fox & Hounds, West Witton:	01969 623650
Palmer Flatt Hotel, Aysgarth Falls:	01969 663228

West Burton Walking Weekend
- Saturday Walk -
West Burton, Carlton Moor, Coverdale, Penhill &
Redmire Force

WALK INFORMATION

Highlights   England's prettiest village, the valley of the Welsh, a long descent into Coverdale, the legend of the giant, waterfalls galore and the wooded banks of the Ure.

Distance   13 miles   Time   6 hours

Maps   OS Explorer OL30

Refreshments   Pubs at West Burton, Carlton, West Witton and Aysgarth Falls. There are shops at West Burton and West Witton, as well as a café at Aysgarth Falls.

Terrain   The section from West Burton to Carlton follows stony / boggy tracks over Carlton Moor, with an initial steep climb up through Thupton Gill. From Carlton, a narrow path leads across Melmerby Moor to join a moorland road for a short distance before a stony track heads off towards Penhill Quarry. There is quite a steep descent across rough pastures into West Witton. The remainder of this walk follows riverside paths back to West Burton, passing a number of impressive waterfalls.

Ascents: Carlton Moor - 485 metres above sea level

Caution   This walk involves a long and steady climb up over Carlton Moor into Coverdale; the route is clear on the ground for most of the way, however, navigation may be difficult in poor weather. Take care when crossing the A684 at Hestholme Bridge.

POINTS OF INTEREST

Walden is a valley of stark beauty, with steep gills cutting deep into the surrounding moorland. This is one of the most remote and least visited valleys in the Dales, mainly due to the fact that only narrow 'dead end' farm lanes wind their way into its upper reaches. Set back from the road near to the entrance to Cote Farm are the remains of an old smelt mill chimney from the lead mining days - the surrounding moors are littered with the remains of lead and coal mines from the 19th Century. The long climb over Carlton Moor is a delight, with wild moorland close at hand and far-reaching views, particularly during the long descent into Coverdale. The many small villages that lie along the length of Coverdale were originally Viking farms situated in small clearings in a forest that once covered the entire dale. This forest was used in Norman times as a hunting forest and Carlton developed as its headquarters where Courts of the Forest were held. The village was also home to Henry Constantine during the 19th Century, a Yorkshire dialect poet known as The Coverdale Bard whose house is identified by an inscription. The Foresters Arms is a classic example of a Dales inn with flagged floors, low beams and open fires. The table in the bar is said to have originally belonged to the monks of Coverham Abbey.

It seems an insult to call Penhill only a hill, for this has all the characteristics of a mountain with towering crags on its northern edge and a windswept summit. Its flat summit, characteristic of many hills in this part of the Yorkshire Dales, is due to the underlying Yoredale Series of rocks which comprise layers of limestone, shales and grits sandwiched together that erode at different rates. This is also a hill of legend. Many years ago an evil giant lived on Penhill and controlled the valley below with a reign of terror. The giant came to a sticky end after a particularly nasty incident where he killed many of the local children. The ghosts of his victims came back to haunt him and, frightened by these spectral figures, he fell to his death from Penhill Crags. This may be the inspiration for West Witton's annual Burning of Bartle, which takes place on or near to the feast of St Bartholomew in late August. Historians are undecided as to the origins of this festival - it may be pagan, later given religious significance through St Bartholomew, or it could be associated with the legend of the Penhill giant or perhaps something more mundane like a sheep-rustler. An effigy of Owd Bartle is paraded around the village then placed on top of a bonfire. From West Witton, this walk follows the banks of the River Ure passing Redmire Force and, further upstream, Aysgarth Falls. These waterfalls have a wonderful setting in a wooded gorge with the wide river cascading over huge shelves of limestone. St Andrew's Church stands proudly above Yore Bridge and the Upper Falls, a wonderful place that boasts the largest churchyard in the country. Dating back to the 12th Century, the Church retains many features including a wooden screen that was carved by the famous Ripon Carvers in 1506 and rescued from Jervaulx Abbey after the Dissolution of the Monasteries. The church was almost entirely rebuilt in the 19th Century, with only the 14th Century tower remaining.

West Burton

WEST BURTON SATURDAY WALK 'MAP A'

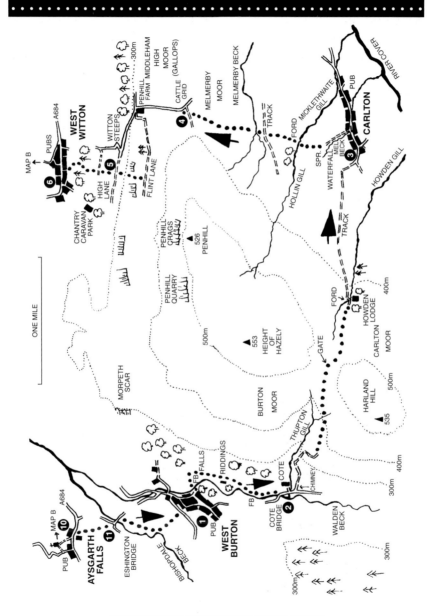

WEST BURTON SATURDAY WALK 'MAP B'

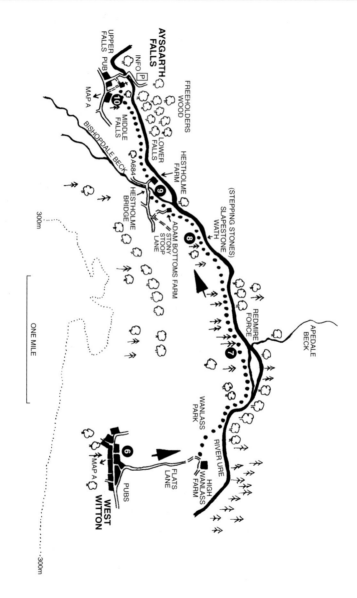

1. With your back to the Fox & Hounds at West Burton, head to the left down across the green to the bottom right-hand corner where a lane leads down beside Mill House to reach West Burton Falls. Cross the packhorse bridge over Walden Beck and follow the path up to the left to a small gate, then head right up the field to another gate adjacent to a barn. Continue heading straight on up the hillside with the stone wall on your right then, where this wall turns away to the right after about 100 yards, head to the right keeping close to the wall / fence (SP 'Rookwith Bridge, Cote Bridge') on to reach a wall-gate. After this wall-gate, head straight on gently rising up to soon join a track which quickly leads up to another wall-gate (beside a gate). Carry straight on across fields through a series of wall-gaps passing Riddings Farm just across to your right after which continue straight on through a further two wall-gaps then head down to the right through a bridlegate in field corner then bear to the left across the next field to reach the FB over Walden Beck (Rookwith Bridge). Do NOT cross this FB but turn left immediately before it (SP 'Cote Bridge') and head straight on along the field perimeter (and Walden Beck) on your right to join a track to the right of a small barn that leads on to join the road beside Cote Bridge.

2. Turn left along the road for a short distance passing the entrance to Cote Farm (and then the driveway to a house) after which take the stony track that branches off to the left past the old smelt mill chimney then climbing steeply up to reach a gate across the track. Head through the gate and continue up along the stony track which levels out slightly for a short distance then bends up to the right then round to the left gradually climbing up, with the ravine of Thupton Gill down to your left, to reach a second gate across the track. After this second gate follow the clear stony track bending sharply to the right alongside the wall / fence on your right then, where this wall turns sharply downhill, follow the grassy track

bending to the left (track levels out). Follow this clear grassy track gradually heading up with Thupton Gill falling away down to your left - the track becomes stony after a while then joins a tumbledown wall on your left which you follow rising up then, where this wall turns sharp left, carry straight on up onto the top of the 'pass' (Carlton Moor) and on to reach a gate in a stone wall, with Height of Hazely to your left and Harland Hill to your right. After the gate, follow the rough path bearing to the right across boggy ground to join a wall on your right which you follow on to reach a gate in the corner of the field, after which carry straight on across the open moorland gently dropping down to join a clear track just to the left-side of Howden Lodge (shooting lodge) hidden in a small stand of trees. Follow this clear stony track heading across open moorland for 0.5 miles to reach a gate at the top of a walled 'green' lane - follow this walled track straight on dropping down into Coverdale for a further 0.75 miles to join a metalled lane which you follow straight on down to reach a T-junction with the main road through Carlton. Turn left at this junction down into the centre of the village.

3. Follow the main road into the centre of the village then, where the road bends slightly to the right after a bridge across Mel Beck, turn left (beside the phone box) and follow the track up passing to the right-hand side of Carlton Methodist Church and through a gate. Follow this track up alongside the small stream on your left then, just after a small waterfall on your left, follow the track through a gate to the right (just before the small stone building). Head straight on along the grassy track heading up to reach a gate to the left of a (roofless) stone barn, after which head to the right across the field (keeping close to the wall on your right) then down along a stony track over a ford across Micklethwaite Gill and up to quickly reach a gate in a fence. Head through this gate then turn immediately left up across the field (no clear path) to soon reach a stile over a fence (marker-post). Cross the stile then head straight on along the narrow path gently rising up across the moorland to join a much clearer path alongside a wall on your right - follow this clear path

straight on (with the wall on your right) to soon reach a gate (open heather moorland ahead). Carry straight on, over a clear shooters' track and follow the wide grassy path straight ahead which soon fords Melmerby Beck - carry straight on along the clear path heading up across the gently rising moorland of Melmerby Moor for 0.75 miles (Penhill up to your left) to reach another shooters' track across your path where you continue straight on to quickly join an unfenced road beside a cattle grid.

4. Turn left over the cattle grid and follow the road down passing the horse gallops of Middleham High Moor on your right then follow the road turning sharp left around Penhill Farm just after which, as you reach the brow of the hill, follow the track off to the left (SP 'Penhill Quarry'). Follow this track on bending sharp left and round to the right then heading straight on passing a small copse of Scots pines on your right after 0.25 miles after which continue along the track for about 400 yards (ignore the first footpath to the right through the small wall-gate at the end of the first field after the Scots pines) then head through the squeeze-stile to the right at the end of the second field on the right after the Scots pines. Head down the field keeping close to the wall on your left zig-zagging down a short but steep bank then on across a flat shelf of land before another short but steep bank and on to reach a squeeze-stile that leads onto the walled track of High Lane.

5. At High Lane, take the footpath opposite to the left (SP 'West Witton') and head down the steep bank keeping close to the small stream on your right to reach a squeeze-stile at the foot of the bank, after which head straight on alongside the wall on your left to reach the walled grassy track of Watery Lane. Head over this track and walk straight on across the next field keeping the tumbledown wall / line of trees on your left, through a wall-gap at the end of this field and on to quickly reach a junction of paths (SP 'Village, Grassgill Lane') where you follow the clear path to the right slanting down through the woods to reach a squeeze-stile at the bottom of the wooded bank. At the end of the woods head straight on across the

field keeping close to the hedge on your right then, as you approach the end of the field beside the gate on your right, bear left (SP 'village') to reach a squeeze-stile in the bottom left corner of the field, then head over the next field through another squeeze-stile that leads onto a enclosed path to emerge onto the small village green opposite the Wensleydale Heifer in the centre of West Witton.

6. Turn right along the main road then take the lane to the left in-between the houses just after the Post Office and village shop (SP 'To the Church'). Follow the road down passing the Church on your right (and old school on your left) then steeply down out of the village to join another lane, which you follow to the left to reach High Wanless Farm after 0.75 miles. Go through the gate (squeeze-stile beside the gate) leading into the farmyard (farmhouse just ahead) then turn immediately left through a metal gate in a wall. After the gate head on bearing slightly to the right across the field to reach a wall gap (75 yards to the right of the gate in the wall), then continue across the field bearing right to reach the steep wooded banks of the River Ure. Head left along the ridge with the river down to the right then, where the wide river bends sharply away, follow the path down the steep bank to join the river. Head straight on across the field bearing very slightly to the left (following the curve of the river round to the left) to join a stone wall and the wooded riverbank on your right. Head up the small grassy bank (alongside the wall on your right) and on across an undulating field then, where the wall curves round to the left, cross a ladder stile over this wall. After the stile, head straight on with the wall and woodland on your right to reach a small gate in the corner of the field on your right (SP). Head through the gate and follow the path down through the woods to reach Redmire Force.

7. As you reach the waterfalls, head up the steps to the left and through a wall gate at the top of the hill, then head straight on along the top of the small grassy ridge and over a wall stile (SP). After the stile head straight on across the field bearing very slightly to the right to reach a ladder stile in the top right corner of the field (with

woodland on your right), then carry straight on alongside the wall on your right (ignore the stiles which lead into the woods) to reach another ladder stile in the corner of the field. Cross the stile and head along the top of a grassy ridge of land (river down to your right) keeping close to the fence on your left, to reach a stile over this fence (where the fence joins a wall). After the stile, turn right to quickly reach a wall stile then head on over another stile across a fence after which head straight on across the field bearing slightly to the right to reach a stile in the far right corner of the field above the wooded banks of the Ure. After the stile turn left through woods and drop down to join a riverside path that leads on to reach the steeping stones and ford at Slapestone Wath.

8. Cross the stile by these stepping stones, then head straight on alongside the river on your right through a series of gates to reach Adam Bottoms Farm. Head straight on skirting around the farm house (ignore the farm track) to reach a gate in a stone wall just beyond the farm. Head straight on through another gate, passing a stone barn (Bishopdale Beck just to your right) to join the main road through a squeeze-stile beside a gate (SP), with Hestholme Bridge just to your right.

9. Turn right along the road over Hestholme Bridge just after which take the footpath to the right at the top of the driveway towards Hestholme Farm (SP). Head diagonally to the right across the field and through a gate in the far right-hand corner after which head on through a small wall-gate that leads onto a clear enclosed path with the wooded banks of the River Ure on your right. Head along this short stretch of enclosed path, over a squeeze-stile after which follow the clear riverside path straight on (waterfalls to your right) through another squeeze-stile that leads onto the riverbank where you follow the path climbing up the bank to the left. At the top of the bank, follow the clear path straight on along the top of the bank passing Lower Falls down to your right, over a stile and bridlegate after which carry on along the bank then, at the corner of the woodland on your right, follow the path climbing up the hillside alongside a tumbledown wall on your right then straight on across a

field to reach a wall-gap in the left-hand corner of the small copse of woodland. Follow the clear path straight on to reach a stile at the other end of the woods, then head straight on down to reach a wall-gate that leads into St Andrews churchyard.

10. Head straight on through the churchyard to reach the tower and entrance porch to the Church where you turn left along the path up through the churchyard then along an enclosed path to reach the main road. Cross the road (take care) and take the footpath directly opposite (SP 'Eshington Bridge') and follow the clear path straight on through a small wall-gate then steeply down into a dip, over a stile (SP) then up to reach another wall-gate. After this wall-gate, head on alongside the stone wall on your left over the brow of the hill (SP) then bear away from the wall to the right through a small gate in a fence. Continue straight on bearing to the left down across the hillside, through a wall-gate (in a section of stone wall) then on to quickly reach another wall-gate after which head straight down the field through a wall-gate beside a large tree (to the left of a gate) that leads onto the road near Eshington Bridge.

11. Turn right along the road over Eshington Bridge, just after which take the footpath to the right (SP 'West Burton') and head straight on across the field to reach a stile. After the stile follow the clear path (Bishopdale Beck to your right) straight on across the field alongside the wall on your right then where this wall bends away continue straight on along the clear path to reach two wall-gaps beside a bend in the river (Bishopdale Beck). After the wall-gaps, head straight on away from the river across the field passing to the right of a barn on to reach a stile by a gate that leads onto the road. Cross the road (take care) and head up the steps opposite and follow the path up between the houses back into West Burton.

West Burton Walking Weekend
- Sunday Walk -
West Burton, West Witton, Morpeth Gate & Hudson Quarry

WALK INFORMATION

Highlights	An ancient road, the chapel of the Knights Templars, wonderful views of Bishopdale, ancient walled tracks, a bird's eye view of West Burton and a hidden waterfall.
Distance	7.5 miles Time 3.5 hours
Maps	OS Explorer OL30
Refreshments	Pubs and shops at West Burton and West Witton.
Terrain	From West Burton, paths leads across fields and through woodland virtually all the way to West Witton, with a walled track and quiet lane as you approach West Witton. A path then climbs quite steeply up to join High Lane, a level walled track which is followed for about 2 miles before climbing steeply up onto Morpeth Scar along the Hudson Quarry track. The final descent into West Burton from this track is steep in places.
Ascents:	Hudson Quarry track - 350 metres above sea level
Caution	This walk involves a number of steep ascents and descents, particularly up to join High Lane and then the descent from the Hudson Quarry track. Keep well away from the edge of Morpeth Scar - sheer drops.

POINTS OF INTEREST

The stone packhorse bridge across Walden Beck leads up through woodland to join a walled track known as Morpeth Gate. This old road, now a stony track, was once a busy route between West Burton and the important market town of Middleham, with its historic castle. It is possible that this was originally a Roman road from the fort at Bainbridge, later used by the Lords of Middleham Castle as a quick route to their hunting forest in Bishopdale. After an initial brief spell along this track, our route heads across pastures following a broad shelf of land with wonderful views across Bishopdale and Wensleydale on to reach the scant ruins of the Chapel of the Knights Templars. This chapel dates from around 1200 and once served a preceptory of the secretive yet powerful Knights Templars; note the tiny stone coffins. The Templars were an international military order whose members were subject to monastic vows. Founded in 1120, their original purpose was to protect pilgrims on their journey to the Holy Land, however they developed into a powerful and wealthy army so much so that Pope Clement V suppressed them in 1312 because they threatened the authority of Rome. After their suppression, the chapel passed into the hands of the Hospitallers, a similar yet less powerful Order. Just up from St Andrews Church at Aysgarth Falls is the Palmer Flatt Hotel, whose unusual name is a reminder of monastic days as it stands on the site of a medieval hospice for pilgrims.

From West Witton, a steep path leads up to re-join Morpeth Gate (also known as High Lane as it passes across the upper slopes of Penhill). This fine walled track heads across a flat shelf of land high above Wensleydale, with superb views across the valley with the menacing crags that scar Penhill's northern edge towering above. Just before the track winds steeply down towards West Burton, another track leads up above Morpeth Scar heading towards Hudson Quarry. This track affords one of the finest views in Wensleydale with a vast panorama across the confluence of the three valleys of Wensleydale, Bishopdale and Walden.

WEST BURTON SUNDAY WALK

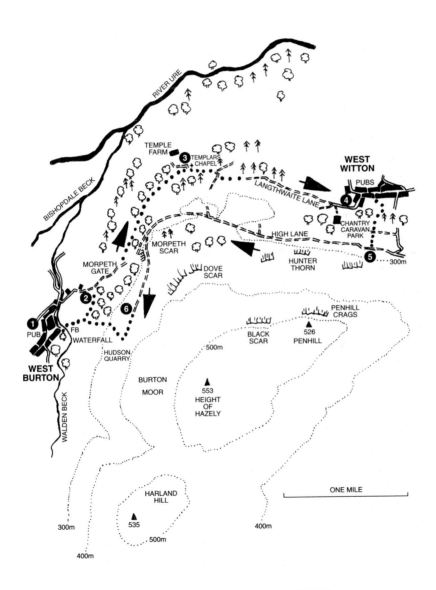

THE WALK

1. Leave West Burton along the lane in the bottom right corner of the green passing Mill House (SP 'Morpeth Gate & Cote Bridge & access to Waterfall') to reach West Burton Force. Head left over the packhorse bridge before the falls and follow the clear path up to the left to reach a small gate, after which turn right along the enclosed path to another gate then head straight up across the field to a stile that leads into woodland (Barrack Wood). Turn left (SP 'Morpeth Lane') and follow the path along the bottom edge of the woods to reach the walled track of Morpeth Gate.

2. Turn right and follow the stony track climbing uphill then levelling out (ignore the path to the left towards 'Temple Farm') before rising up again then, halfway up this hill, take the path to the left through a gate (SP 'Templars Chapel'). Follow the clear path straight on with the wall / fence on your left then, as the field narrows, follow the clear path bearing up to the right (SP) to a gate at the end of a section of stone wall. After the gate head straight on keeping close to the fence / wall on your left over a series of stiles heading across a flat shelf of land, with the steep wooded slope to your left, following the hillside as it gently curves round to the right to eventually reach the top of a walled track, just beyond which are the ruins of the Templars Chapel.

3. Turn right through the gate at the top of the walled track (SP 'Nossill Lane via Langthwaite Lane') then bear to the left across the field to join a rough track that leads to a gate in a wall between the two woods on the hillside. Head through the gate and follow the rough track up to join a concrete lane across your path. Turn right up along this lane for a short distance then, where this lane bends up to the right, head straight on along the grassy path (SP 'Nossill Lane via Langthwaite Lane') up over the brow of the hill to reach a gate in a stone wall. Head left through the gate then walk straight on across the field and through the left-hand of two gates in the stone

wall across your path. After the gate, walk straight on alongside the wall on your right then, halfway along this field, head right over a wall-stile (SP) that leads onto the top of the walled track of Langthwaite Lane. Turn left and follow this walled grassy track straight on for about 0.75 miles to join a metalled lane, which you follow to the left down to reach the main road in the centre of West Witton.

4. Turn right along the main road passing the small village green on your right immediately after which (opposite the Wensleydale Heifer Inn) turn right (SP 'Moor Bank') passing to the side of a house (with the green on your right) to reach an enclosed path to the left just behind the house beside the small pond. Follow this enclosed path up to reach a wall-gate on the edge of the village (with fields ahead) then head to the left across the field and through a squeeze-stile after which head across the next field to join the hedge / fence on the opposite side which you follow up to the right (SP 'Kagram, High Lane') to reach a squeeze-stile at the foot of a steep wooded bank. Follow the clear path slanting to the right up across the wooded bank, at the top of which head through the squeeze-stile just to the left (SP 'Watery Lane, High Lane'). After the squeeze-stile head straight on alongside the line of trees / tumbledown wall on to reach an old walled grassy track (watery Lane). Head over this track through the wall-gate ahead then head straight up the field keeping close to the wall on your right to reach a squeeze-stile in the top right-hand corner at the foot of a steep bank, after which head straight up the grassy bank along the right-hand side of the small stream to reach a wall-gate that leads onto the walled stony track of High Lane.

5. Turn right along this clear stony track and follow it straight on for 2 miles heading across a flat shelf of land on the lower flanks of Penhill (ignore any turnings off this main walled track) - after about 1.5 miles the track begins to gently drop down (flat-topped Addlebrough and the hills of Upper Wensleydale come into view ahead) then gradually bends round to the left following the curve of

the hillside to reach a fork in the stony track (with the limestone crags of Morpeth Scar ahead). Follow the left-hand track (SP 'West Burton via Hudson Quarry Lane') climbing up alongside the wall on your left (do not head down the clearer track to the right) up to the top of Morpeth Scar (keep away from the edge - sheer drops). Carry straight on along the clear track, which soon levels out and becomes a walled grassy track which you follow on to reach a ladder stile beside a gate at the end of the walled track.

6. Head through the gate and continue along the clear grassy track keeping close to the wall on your left heading across a flat shelf of land then, where the wall on your left ends and a wall begins on your right, turn sharp right along a clear narrow path heading down the hillside (SP 'West Burton'), bearing very slightly to the right down across a number of small 'ridges' to reach a wall-gate at the top of a steep bank. Head through the wall-gate and follow the clear path zig-zagging down across the steep hillside, over a tumbledown wall at the bottom of the steep bank then bear slightly to the right to reach a stile that leads into woodland. Follow the clear path to the left down through the trees, through an old squeeze-stile that leads into Barrack Wood then carry on alongside the fence on your left (along the edge of the wood) to soon reach a stile over this fence to your left (SP) where the fence curves round to the right. Cross this stile and head straight down the field to reach a gate to the left of a stone barn that leads onto an enclosed path which you follow back down to reach the stone packhorse bridge near West Burton Falls and back into West Burton.

For an alternative walk from West Burton (taking in Aysgarth and Bishopdale) please see Walking Weekend 2